T0326375

THE NEXT REVOLUTION

THE NEXT REVOLUTION

Popular Assemblies and the
Promise of Direct Democracy

———————◆———————

Essays by Murray Bookchin

*Edited and with an Introduction by
Debbie Bookchin and Blair Taylor*

Foreword by Ursula K. Le Guin

VERSO

London • New York

First published by Verso 2015
© The Murray Bookchin Trust 2015
Foreword © Ursula K. Le Guin 2015
Introduction © Debbie Bookchin and Blair Taylor 2015

1 3 5 7 9 10 8 6 4 2

Verso
UK: 6 Meard Street, London W1F 0EG
US: 388 Atlantic Ave, Brooklyn, NY 11217
www.versobooks.com

Verso is the imprint of New Left Books

ISBN-13: 978-1-78168-581-5 (PB)
ISBN-13: 978-1-78168-580-8 (HC)
eISBN-13: 978-1-78168-582-2 (US)
eISBN-13: 978-1-78168-733-8 (UK)

British Library Cataloguing in Publication Data
A catalogue record for this book is available from the British Library

Library of Congress Cataloging-in-Publication Data

Bookchin, Murray, 1921–2006.
The next revolution / Murray Bookchin, Debbie Bookchin, Blair Taylor ;
preface by Ursula K. Le Guin.
  pages cm
ISBN 978-1-78168-581-5 (paperback)
1. Political participation. 2. Direct democracy. I. Bookchin, Debbie.
II. Taylor, Blair. III. Title.
JF799.B67 2015
321.8—dc23
                    2014029113

Typeset in Adobe Garamond by Hewer Text UK Ltd, Edinburgh, Scotland
Printed in the US

For Bea Bookchin

confidante, intellectual partner,
and dearest friend to Murray Bookchin
for more than fifty years

Contents

Foreword
By Ursula K. Le Guin

"The Left," a meaningful term ever since the French Revolution, took on wider significance with the rise of socialism, anarchism, and communism. The Russian revolution installed a government entirely leftist in conception; leftist and rightist movements tore Spain apart; democratic parties in Europe and North America arrayed themselves between the two poles; liberal cartoonists portrayed the opposition as a fat plutocrat with a cigar, while reactionaries in the United States demonized "commie leftists" from the 1930s through the Cold War. The left/right opposition, though often an oversimplification, for two centuries was broadly useful as a description and a reminder of dynamic balance.

In the twenty-first century we go on using the terms, but what is left of the Left? The failure of state communism, the quiet entrenchment of a degree of socialism in democratic governments, and the relentless rightward movement of politics driven by corporate capitalism have made much progressive thinking seem antiquated, or redundant, or illusory. The Left is marginalized in its thought, fragmented in its goals, unconfident of its ability to unite. In America particularly, the drift to the right has been so strong that mere liberalism is now the terrorist bogey that anarchism or socialism used to be, and reactionaries are called "moderates."

So, in a country that has all but shut its left eye and is trying to use only its right hand, where does an ambidextrous, binocular Old Rad like Murray Bookchin fit?

I think he'll find his readers. A lot of people are seeking consistent, constructive thinking on which to base action—a frustrating search. Theoretical approaches that seem promising turn out, like the Libertarian Party, to be Ayn Rand in drag; immediate and effective solutions to a problem turn out, like the Occupy movement, to lack structure and stamina for the long run. Young people, people this society blatantly short changes and betrays, are looking for intelligent, realistic, long-term thinking: not another ranting ideology, but a practical working hypothesis, a methodology of how to regain control of where we're going. Achieving that control will require a revolution as powerful, as deeply affecting society as a whole, as the force it wants to harness.

Murray Bookchin was an expert in nonviolent revolution. He thought about radical social changes, planned and unplanned, and how best to prepare for them, all his life. This book carries his thinking on past his own life into the threatening future we face.

Impatient, idealistic readers may find him uncomfortably toughminded. He's unwilling to leap over reality to dreams of happy endings, unsympathetic to mere transgression pretending to be political action: "A 'politics' of disorder or 'creative chaos,' or a naïve practice of 'taking over the streets' (usually little more than a street festival), regresses participants to the behavior of a juvenile herd." That applies more to the Summer of Love, certainly, than to the Occupy movement, yet it is a permanently cogent warning. But Bookchin is no grim puritan. I first read him as an anarchist, probably the most eloquent and thoughtful one of his generation, and in moving away from anarchism he hasn't lost his sense of the joy of freedom. He doesn't want to see that joy, that freedom, come crashing down, yet again, among the ruins of its own euphoric irresponsibility.

What all political and social thinking has finally been forced to face is, of course, the irreversible degradation of the environment by unrestrained industrial capitalism: the enormous fact of which science has been trying for fifty years to convince us, while technology provided us ever greater distractions from it. Every benefit industrialism and capitalism have brought us, every wonderful advance in knowledge and health and communication and comfort, casts the same fatal shadow. All we have, we have taken from the earth; and, taking with ever-increasing speed and greed, we now return little but what is sterile or poisoned. Yet we can't stop the process. A capitalist economy, by definition, lives by growth; as he observes: "For capitalism to desist from its mindless expansion would be for it to commit social suicide." We have, essentially, chosen cancer as the model of our social system.

Capitalism's grow-or-die imperative stands radically at odds with ecology's imperative of interdependence and limit. The two imperatives can no longer coexist with each other; nor can any society founded on the myth that they can be reconciled hope to survive. Either we will establish an ecological society or society will go under for everyone, irrespective of his or her status.

Murray Bookchin spent a lifetime opposing the rapacious ethos of grow-or-die capitalism. The nine essays in this book represent the culmination of that labor: the theoretical underpinning for an egalitarian and directly democratic ecological society, with a practical approach for how to build it. He critiques the failures of past movements for social change, resurrects the promise of direct democracy and, in the last essay in this book, sketches his hope of how we might turn the environmental crisis into a moment of true choice—a chance to transcend the paralyzing hierarchies of gender, race, class, nation, a chance to find a radical cure for the radical evil of our social system. Reading it, I was moved and grateful, as I have so often been in reading Murray Bookchin. He was a true son of the Enlightenment in his respect for clear thought and moral responsibility and in his honest, uncompromising search for a realistic hope.

Introduction

The world today confronts not one, but a series of interlocking crises—economic, political, social, and ecological. The new millennium has been marked by a growing gap between rich and poor that has reached unprecedented levels of disparity, consigning an entire generation to diminished expectations and dismal prospects. Socially, the trajectory of the new century has been equally bleak, particularly in the developing world, where sectarian violence in the name of religion, tribalism, and nationalism has turned entire regions into insufferable battle zones. Meanwhile, the environmental crisis has worsened at a pace that has exceeded even the most pessimistic forecasts. Global warming, rising sea levels, pollution of the air, soil, and oceans, and the destruction of massive tracts of rain forest have accelerated at such alarming rates that the environmental catastrophe that was expected to reach grave proportions sometime in the next century has instead become the pressing, urgent concern of this generation.

Yet, in the face of these ever-worsening crises, the perverse logic of neoliberal capitalism is so entrenched that, despite its spectacular collapse in 2008, the only thinkable response has been more neoliberalism: an ever-increasing deference to corporate and financial elites, which posits privatization, slashing services, and giving free reign to the market as the only way out. The result has been a predictable rise in disenfranchisement politically and an electoral politics devoid of substantive debate and choice—an exercise in showmanship—whether in Argentina, Italy, Germany, or the United States. Still, while political and economic elites insist "there is no alternative" and cynically double down on the status quo of austerity, activists around the world have challenged this conventional wisdom with a new politics, demanding a more expansive form of democracy. From New York and Cairo to Istanbul and Rio, movements like Occupy Wall Street and the Spanish *indignados* have pried open new space with an exciting politics that defies existing categories, attacking both capitalist inequality and ossified "representative" democracies. The voices and demands are diverse, but at their root is a direct challenge to the current political ethos in which the economic and social policies of elected governments— left, right, or center—have blurred into an indistinguishable consensus of tinkering around the edges and unquestioning obeisance to global market capitalism. These movements have ignited widespread excitement, attracting millions of participants around the world to massive rallies, and have kindled once again the hope that from the streets will arise the flame of a revolutionary new social movement.

Despite inspired moments of resistance, the radical democracy forged in squares from Zuccotti to Taksim has still not congealed into a viable political alternative. The excitement and solidarity on the ground has yet to coalesce into a political praxis capable of eliminating the current array of repressive forces and replacing it with a visionary, egalitarian—and importantly, achievable—new society. Murray Bookchin directly addresses this need, offering a transformative vision and new political strategy for a truly free society—a project that he called "Communalism."

A prolific author, essayist and activist, Bookchin devoted his life to developing a new kind of left politics that speaks to both movement concerns and the diverse social problems they confront. Communalism moves beyond critique to offer a reconstructive vision of a fundamentally different society—directly democratic,

anticapitalist, ecological, and opposed to all forms of domination—
that actualizes freedom in popular assemblies bound together in
confederation. Rescuing the revolutionary project from the taint of
authoritarianism and the supposed "end of history," Communalism
advances a bold politics that moves from resistance to social
transformation.

Bookchin's use of the term Communalism signifies his arrival,
after six decades as an activist and theorist, at a philosophy of social
change that was shaped by a lifetime on the left. Born in 1921, he
became radicalized at the age of nine, when he joined the Young
Pioneers, the Communist youth organization in New York City.
He became a Trotskyist in the late thirties and, beginning in 1948,
spent a decade in the libertarian socialist Contemporary Issues
group, which had abandoned orthodox Marxist ideology. In the late
1950s, he began to elaborate the importance of environmental degradation as a symptom of deeply entrenched social problems.
Bookchin's book on the subject, *Our Synthetic Environment,*
appeared six months before Rachel Carson's *Silent Spring,* while his
seminal 1964 pamphlet *Ecology and Revolutionary Thought* introduced the concept of ecology as a political category to the New Left.
That essay's groundbreaking synthesis of anarchism, ecology, and
decentralization was the first to equate the grow-or-die logic of
capitalism with the ecological destruction of the planet and presented a profound new understanding of capitalism's impact on the
environment as well as social relations. His 1968 essay "Post-Scarcity
Anarchism" reformulated anarchist theory for a new era, providing
a coherent framework for the reorganization of society along eco-
logical-anarchistic lines. As Students for a Democratic Society
(SDS) was imploding into Marxist sectarianism at its final convention in 1969, Bookchin was distributing his pamphlet *Listen
Marxist!,* which criticized the retrogressive return to dogmatic
Marxism by various factions of SDS. He advocated for an alternative anarchist politics of direct democracy and decentralization,
ideas that were buried in the rubble of the crumbling organization
but which resonated with those movements that would later become

dominant on the left. His essays from this period, originally published in the magazine *Anarchos* by a New York City group that Bookchin cofounded in the mid-1960s, were collected in the 1971 anthology *Post-Scarcity Anarchism*, a book that exerted a profound influence on the New Left and became a classic articulation of twentieth-century anarchism.

Authoring twenty-three works of history, political theory, philosophy, and urban studies, Bookchin drew on a rich intellectual tradition that ranged from Aristotle, Hegel, and Marx to Karl Polanyi, Hans Jonas, and Lewis Mumford. In his major work, *The Ecology of Freedom* (1982), he elaborated the historical, anthropological, and social roots of hierarchy and domination and their implications for our relationship to the natural world in an expansive theory that he called "social ecology." He challenged and influenced every major figure of the period, from Noam Chomsky and Herbert Marcuse to Daniel Cohn-Bendit and Guy Debord.

In 1974, Bookchin cofounded the Institute for Social Ecology (ISE), a unique educational project in Vermont offering classes in political theory, radical history, and practical ecological initiatives like organic agriculture and solar energy. He was an important influence on the overlapping tendencies of nonviolent direct action, peace, radical feminism, and ecology that comprised the new social movements of the late 1970s and 1980s. Drawing on his own activist background as, variously, a young street agitator, autoworker shop steward, and civil rights organizer for CORE (the Congress of Racial Equality), he played a leadership role in the antinuclear Clamshell Alliance and in the formation of the Left Green Network. In her book *Political Protest and Cultural Revolution: Nonviolent Direct Action in the 1970s and 1980s*, Barbara Epstein credits Bookchin with introducing the concept of affinity groups and popularizing the European Critical Theory of Theodor Adorno and Max Horkheimer. His ideas of face-to-face participatory democracy, general assemblies, and confederation were adopted as the basic modes of organization and decision-making by much of the antinuclear movement worldwide and later by the alterglobalization movement, which employed them to ensure democracy in their organization and decision-making processes. Bookchin also met and corresponded with German Green leaders and was a key voice in the *Realo/Fundi* debate over whether the Greens should remain a movement or become a conventional party. His work had a global reach and was widely translated and reprinted throughout Europe, Latin America, and Asia.

In the 1980s and 1990s, Bookchin was a central interlocutor for critical theorists like Cornelius Castoriadis and a frequent contributor to the influential journal *Telos*. He engaged in lively debates with prominent ecological thinkers like Arne Ness and David Foreman. Meanwhile, the Institute for Social Ecology played an important role in the alterglobalization movement that emerged in Seattle in 1999, becoming a space for activist reflection while advocating direct democracy and anticapitalism in contrast to the reformist, anticorporate discourse of many NGOs, and launched a variety of left libertarian and ecological initiatives. But by the mid-1990s, problematic tendencies within some strains of anarchism toward primitivism, lifestyle politics, and aversion to organization led Bookchin first to try to reclaim a social anarchism before eventually breaking with the tradition entirely. Reflecting on a lifetime of experience on the left, Bookchin spent the last fifteen years before his death in 2006 working on a comprehensive four-volume study of revolutionary history called *The Third Revolution*, in which he offered astute conclusions about the failure of revolutionary movements—from peasant uprisings to modern insurrections—to effect lasting social change. These insights informed a new political perspective, one he hoped could avoid the pitfalls of the past and lead to a new, emancipatory praxis—Communalism.

It was during this period that Bookchin published many of the essays contained in this collection, formally elaborating the concept of Communalism and its concrete political dimension, libertarian municipalism. Communalist politics suggests a way out of the familiar deadlock between the anarchist and Marxist traditions, offering a missing third pole in the recent debate between Simon

Critchley and Slavoj Žižek. Rejecting both the modesty of Critchley's purely defensive politics of resistance as well as Žižek's obsession with the seizure of oppressive state power, Bookchin instead returns to the recurrent formation arising in nearly every revolutionary upsurge: popular assemblies. From the *quartiers* of the Paris Commune to the general assemblies of Occupy Wall Street and elsewhere, these self-organized democratic councils run like a red thread through history up to the present. Yet revolutionaries of all stripes have largely overlooked the broader potential of these popular institutions. Subjected to centralized party discipline by Marxists and viewed with suspicion by anarchists, these institutions of popular power, which Hannah Arendt called the "lost treasure" of the revolutionary tradition, are the foundation of Bookchin's political project. Communalism develops this recurring historical form into the basis for a comprehensive libertarian socialist vision of direct democracy.

One of Bookchin's early formulations of libertarian municipalism appeared in 1987, when he wrote *The Rise of Urbanization and the Decline of Citizenship* (republished later as *From Urbanization to Cities*), a follow-up to his earlier book *The Limits of the City* (1971), in which he traced the history of the urban megalopolis and argued for decentralization. In the later volume, Bookchin revisited the history of the city to explain the importance of an empowered citizenry as the fundamental basis for creating free communities. He distinguished "statecraft," in which individuals have a diminished influence in political affairs because of the limits of representational government, from "politics," in which citizens have direct, participatory control over their governments and communities. The ideas contained in this book, in which Bookchin returns to the Greek polis to flesh out notions of face-to-face participatory democracy, general assemblies, and confederation, offer a prefigurative strategy in which a new society is created in the shell of the old. This concept of direct democracy has played a growing role in the libertarian leftism of activists today and has become the fundamental organizational principle of Occupy Wall Street, even if many of its adherents were unaware of its origins. As David Harvey observed in his book *Rebel Cities*, "Bookchin's proposal is by far the most sophisticated radical proposal to deal with the creation and collective use of the commons across a wide variety of scales."

The nine essays here offer an excellent overview of Bookchin's political philosophy and the most mature formulation of his thinking with respect to the forms of organization necessary to develop a countervailing force to the coercive power of the nation-state. Each was originally written as a stand-alone work; in collecting them for this volume we have edited the essays where necessary to avoid excessive repetition and preserve clarity. Taken together, they challenge us to accomplish the changes necessary to save our planet and achieve real human freedom, and offer a concrete program by which to accomplish this sweeping social transformation. The writings in this collection serve as both an introduction and culmination to the work of one of the most original thinkers of the twentieth century.

In the opening essay, "The Communalist Project," Bookchin situates Communalism vis-à-vis other left ideologies, arguing that the world has changed significantly from the times that birthed anarchism and Marxism; he contends that these older ideologies are no longer capable of addressing the new and highly generalized problems posed by the modern world, from global warming to postindustrialization. The second essay, "The Ecological Crisis and the Need to Remake Society," elucidates the core insight of Bookchin's social ecology—that the ecological and social crises are intertwined, indeed, that our domination of nature is a projection of domination of human by human in society. Rejecting ecological arguments that blame individual choices, technology, or population growth, Bookchin argues that the ecological crisis is caused by an irrational social system governed by the cancerous logic of capitalism, driven by its competitive grow-or-die imperative and its endless production directed not toward meeting human needs but accumulating profit. Arguing against the extremes of an authoritarian state or totally autonomous self-sufficiency, Bookchin offers

Communalism as an emancipatory alternative capable of saving
ourselves and nature at the same time.

The three middle essays, "A Politics for the Twenty-First Century,"
"The Meaning of Confederalism," and "Libertarian Municipalism: A
Politics of Direct Democracy," describe in detail different aspects of
libertarian municipalism. The first outlines how confederated assemblies can assert popular control over the economy in order to abolish
it as a separate social realm, directing it to human needs rather than
profit. "The Meaning of Confederalism" further elaborates on these
themes and addresses specific objections to the concept of confederal
direct democracy. It answers common questions such as, Is confederation feasible in a globalized world? How would local assemblies
address bigger problems in a democratic manner? Would local communities cooperate or compete with each other, or could localism
devolve to parochialism? "Libertarian Municipalism: A Politics of
Direct Democracy" traces the familiar historical trajectory from
movements into parties—social democratic, socialist, and Green
alike—which have consistently failed to change the world but instead
are changed by it. By contrast, libertarian municipalism changes not
only the content but also the *form* of politics, transforming politics
from its current lowly status as what reviled politicians do *to* us into
a new paradigm in which politics is something we, as fully engaged
citizens, do for ourselves, thus reclaiming democratic control over our
own lives and communities.

Exploring the unique liberatory potential of the city and the
citizen throughout history, "Cities: The Unfolding of Reason in
History" examines the degradation of the concept of "citizen"—
from that of a free individual empowered to participate and make
collective decisions to a mere constituent and taxpayer. Bookchin
seeks to rescue the Enlightenment notion of a progressive, but not
teleological, concept of History wherein reason guides human
action toward the eradication of toil and oppression; or put posi-
tively, freedom.

The essays "Nationalism and the 'National Question'" and
"Anarchism and Power in the Spanish Revolution" elucidate a

libertarian perspective on questions of power, cultural identity, and political sovereignty. In the former, Bookchin places nationalism in the larger historical context of humanity's social evolution, with the aim of transcending it, suggesting instead a libertarian and cosmopolitan ethics of complementarity in which cultural differences serve to enhance human unity. In "Anarchism and Power in the Spanish Revolution" he confronts the question of power, describing how anarchists throughout history have seen power as an essentially negative evil that must be destroyed. Bookchin contends that power will always exist, but that the question revolutionaries face is whether it will rest in the hands of elites or be given an emancipatory institutional form.

The concluding, previously unpublished, essay "The Future of the Left" assesses the fate of the revolutionary project during the twentieth century, examining the Marxist and anarchist traditions. Bookchin argues that Marxism remains trapped by a limited focus on economy and is deeply marred by its legacy of authoritarian statism. Anarchism, by contrast, retains a problematic individualism that valorizes abstract and liberal notions of "autonomy" over a more expansive notion of freedom, ducking thorny questions about collective power, social institutions, and political strategy. Communalism resolves this tension by giving freedom concrete institutional form in confederated popular assemblies. The essay concludes with a passionate defense of the Enlightenment and a reminder that its legacy of discerning the "is" from the "ought" still constitutes the very core of the Left: critique directed toward unlocking the potentiality of universal human freedom.

Today, few deny the grim reality of overlapping political, economic, and ecological crises that currently confront the world. Yet, despite inspiring moments of popular outrage and mobilization, no viable alternative social vision has emerged; hypercompetition, austerity, and ecological degradation march on, opposed yet also unstopped. The present exhaustion of conventional politics calls for bold new ideas that speak to the radically democratic aspirations at the core of contemporary global movements. Bookchin's

Communalism circumvents the stalemate between the state and the street—the familiar oscillation between empowering but ephemeral street protest and entering the very state institutions designed to uphold the present order. He expands our horizons from endlessly opposing the venality of politicians and corporate power to a new organization of society, which redefines politics from a detested thing done to us to something we do ourselves, together, giving substance to the term "freedom" by allowing us to take control of our lives. Bookchin offers a vision of what such a truly free society might look like, and a road map capable of transporting us there. Therefore, we offer this book with the hope that the ideas do not lie dormant on the page, but inspire thought and action that enables us to move from resistance to social transformation.

Debbie Bookchin and Blair Taylor

1

The Communalist Project

Whether the twenty-first century will be the most radical of times or the most reactionary—or will simply lapse into a gray era of dismal mediocrity—will depend overwhelmingly upon the kind of social movement and program that social radicals create out of the theoretical, organizational, and political wealth that has accumulated during the past two centuries of the revolutionary era. The direction we select, from among several intersecting roads of human development, may well determine the future of our species for centuries to come. As long as this irrational society endangers us with nuclear and biological weapons, we cannot ignore the possibility that the entire human enterprise may come to a devastating end. Given the exquisitely elaborate technical plans that the military-industrial complex has devised, the self-extermination of the human species must be included in the futuristic scenarios that, at the turn of the millennium, the mass media are projecting—the end of a human future as such.

Lest these remarks seem too apocalyptic, I should emphasize that we also live in an era when human creativity, technology, and imagination have the capability to produce extraordinary material achievements and to endow us with societies that allow for a degree of freedom that far and away exceeds the most dramatic and emancipatory visions projected by social theorists such as Saint-Simon,

Charles Fourier, Karl Marx, and Peter Kropotkin.[1] Many thinkers of the postmodern age have obtusely singled out science and technology as the principal threats to human well-being, yet few disciplines have imparted to humanity such a stupendous knowledge of the innermost secrets of matter and life, or provided our species better with the ability to alter every important feature of reality and to improve the well-being of human and nonhuman life forms.

We are thus in a position either to follow a path toward a grim "end of history," in which a banal succession of vacuous events replaces genuine progress, or to move on to a path toward the true making of history, in which humanity genuinely progresses toward a rational world. We are in a position to choose between an ignominious finale, possibly including the catastrophic nuclear oblivion of history itself, and history's rational fulfillment in a free, materially abundant society in an aesthetically crafted environment.

Precisely at a time when we, as a species, are capable of producing the means for amazing objective advances and improvements in the human condition and in the nonhuman natural world—advances that could make for a free and rational society—we stand almost naked morally before the onslaught of social forces that may very well lead to our physical immolation. Prognoses about the future are understandably very fragile and are easily distrusted. Pessimism has become widespread, as capitalist social relations become more deeply entrenched in the human mind than ever before and as culture regresses appallingly, almost to a vanishing point.

Having brought history to a point where nearly everything is

---

1   Many less well-known names could be added to this list, but one that in particular I would like very much to single out is the gallant leader of the Left Socialist Revolutionary Party, Maria Spiridonova, whose supporters were virtually alone in proposing a workable revolutionary program for the Russian people in 1917–18. Their failure to implement their political insights and replace the Bolsheviks (with whom they initially joined in forming the first Soviet government) not only led to their defeat but contributed to the disastrous failure of revolutionary movements in the century that followed.

possible, at least of a material nature—and having left behind a past that was permeated ideologically by mystical and religious elements produced by the human imagination—we are faced with a new challenge, one that has never before confronted humanity. We must consciously create our own world, not according to mindless customs and destructive prejudices, but according to the canons of *reason, reflection,* and *discourse* that uniquely belong to our own species.

What factors should be decisive going forward? Of great significance is the immense accumulation of social and political experience that is available to activists today, a storehouse of knowledge that, properly conceived, could be used to avoid the terrible errors that our predecessors made and to spare humanity the terrible plagues of failed revolutions in the past. Also, of indispensable importance is the potential for a new theoretical springboard that has been created by the history of ideas, one that provides the means to catapult an emerging radical movement beyond existing social conditions into a future that fosters humanity's emancipation.

But we must also be fully aware of the scope of the problems that we face. We must understand with complete clarity where we stand in the development of the prevailing capitalist order, and we have to grasp emergent social problems and address them in the program of a new movement. Capitalism is unquestionably the most dynamic society ever to appear in history. By definition, to be sure, it always remains a system of commodity exchange in which objects that are made for sale and profit pervade and mediate most human relations. Yet capitalism is also a highly mutable system, continually advancing the brutal maxim that whatever enterprise does not grow at the expense of its rivals must die. Hence, "growth" and perpetual change become the very laws of life of capitalist existence. This means that capitalism never remains permanently in only one form; it must always transform the institutions that arise from its basic social relations.

Although capitalism became a dominant society only in the past few centuries, it long existed on the periphery of earlier societies: in a largely commercial form, structured around trade between cities and empires; in a craft form throughout the European Middle Ages; in a hugely industrial form in our own time; and if we are to believe recent seers, in an informational form in the coming period. It has created not only new technologies but also a great variety of economic and social structures, such as the small shop, the factory, the huge mill, and the industrial and commercial complex. Certainly the capitalism of the Industrial Revolution has not completely disappeared, any more than the isolated peasant family and small craftsman of a still earlier period have been consigned to complete oblivion. Much of the past is always incorporated into the present; as Marx insistently warned, there is no "pure capitalism," and none of the earlier forms of capitalism fade away until radically new social relations are established and become overwhelmingly dominant. But today, capitalism, even as it coexists with and utilizes precapitalist institutions for its own ends, now reaches into the suburbs and the countryside with its shopping malls and newly styled factories. Indeed, it is by no means inconceivable that one day it will reach beyond our planet. In any case, it has produced not only new commodities to create and feed new wants but new social and cultural issues, which in turn have given rise to new supporters and antagonists of the existing system. The famous first part of Marx and Engels's *Communist Manifesto*, in which they celebrate capitalism's wonders, would have to be periodically rewritten to keep pace with the achievements—as well as the horrors—produced by the bourgeoisie's development.

One of the most striking features of capitalism today is that in the Western world the highly simplified two-class structure—the bourgeoisie and the proletariat—that Marx and Engels predicted would become dominant under "mature" capitalism has undergone a process of reconfiguration. The conflict between wage labor and capital, while it has by no means disappeared, nonetheless lacks the all-embracing importance that it possessed in the past. Contrary to Marx's expectations, the industrial working class is now dwindling in numbers and is steadily losing its traditional identity as a class, which by no means excludes it from a potentially broader and perhaps more extensive conflict of society as a whole against capitalist social relations. Present-day culture, social relations, cityscapes, modes of production, agriculture, and transportation have remade the traditional proletarian into a largely petty bourgeois stratum whose mentality is marked by its own utopianism of "consumption for the sake of consumption." We can foresee a time when the proletarian, whatever the color of his or her collar or place on the assembly line, will be completely replaced by automated and even miniaturized means of production that are operated by a few white-coated manipulators of machines and by computers.

Seen as a whole, the social condition that capitalism has produced today stands very much at odds with the simplistic class prognoses advanced by Marx and by the revolutionary French syndicalists. After the Second World War, capitalism underwent an enormous transformation, creating broad new social issues with extraordinary rapidity, issues that went beyond traditional proletarian demands for improved wages, hours, and working conditions: notably, environmental, gender, hierarchical, civic, and democratic issues. Capitalism, in effect, has generalized its threats to humanity, particularly with climatic changes that may alter the very face of the planet, oligarchical institutions of a global scope, and rampant urbanization that radically corrodes the civic life basic to grassroots politics.

Hierarchy, today, is becoming as pronounced an issue as class, as witness the extent to which many social analyses have singled out managers, bureaucrats, scientists, and the like as emerging, ostensibly dominant groups. New and elaborate gradations of status and interests count today to an extent that they did not in the recent past; they blur the conflict between wage labor and capital that was once so central, clearly defined, and militantly waged by traditional socialists. Class categories are now intermingled with hierarchical categories based on race, gender, sexual preference, and certainly national or regional differences. Status differentiations,

characteristic of hierarchy, tend to converge with class differentiations, and a more all-inclusive capitalistic world is emerging in
which ethnic, national, and gender differences often surpass the
importance of class differences in the public eye.

At the same time, capitalism has produced a new, perhaps paramount contradiction: the clash between an economy based on
unending growth and the desiccation of the natural environment.[2]
This issue and its vast ramifications can no more be minimized, let
alone dismissed, than the need of human beings for food or air. At
present, the most promising struggles in the West, where socialism
was born, seem to be waged less around income and working conditions than around nuclear power, pollution, deforestation, urban
blight, education, health care, community life, and the oppression of
people in underdeveloped countries—as witness the (albeit sporadic)
antiglobalization upsurges, in which blue- and white-collar "workers"
march in the same ranks with middle-class humanitarians and are
motivated by common social concerns. Proletarian combatants
become indistinguishable from middle-class ones. Burly workers,
whose hallmark is a combative militancy, now march behind "bread
and puppet" theater performers, often with a considerable measure of
shared playfulness. Members of the working and middle classes now
wear many different social hats, so to speak, challenging capitalism
obliquely as well as directly on cultural as well as economic grounds.

Nor can we ignore, in deciding what direction we are to follow,
the fact that capitalism, if it is not checked, will in the future—and
not necessarily the very distant future—differ appreciably from the
system we know today. Capitalist development can be expected to
vastly alter the social horizon in the years ahead. Can we suppose that
factories, offices, cities, residential areas, industry, commerce, and
agriculture, let alone moral values, aesthetics, media, popular desires,

---

2 I frankly regard this contradiction as more fundamental than the
often-indiscernible tendency of the rate of profit to decline and thereby to render
capitalist exchange inoperable—a contradiction to which Marxists assigned a
decisive role in the nineteenth and early twentieth centuries.

and the like will not change immensely before the twenty-first century is out? In the past century, capitalism, above all else, has broadened social issues—indeed, the historical social question of how a humanity, divided by classes and exploitation, will create a society based on equality, the development of authentic harmony, and freedom—to include those whose resolution was barely foreseen by the liberatory social theorists in the nineteenth and early twentieth centuries. Our age, with its endless array of "bottom lines" and "investment choices," now threatens to turn society itself into a vast and exploitative marketplace.[3]

Given the changes that we are witnessing and those that are still taking form, social radicals can no longer oppose the predatory (as well as immensely creative) capitalist system by using the ideologies and methods that were born in the first Industrial Revolution, when a factory proletarian seemed to be the principal antagonist of a textile plant owner. Nor can we use ideologies that were spawned by conflicts that an impoverished peasantry used to oppose feudal and semifeudal landowners. None of the professedly anticapitalist ideologies of the past—Marxism, anarchism, syndicalism, and more generic forms of socialism—retain the same relevance that they had at an earlier stage of capitalist development and in an earlier period of technological advance. Nor can any of them hope to encompass the multitude of new issues, opportunities, problems, and interests that capitalism has repeatedly created over time.

---

3 Contrary to Marx's assertion that a society disappears only when it has exhausted its capacity for new technological developments, capitalism is in a state of permanent technological revolution—at times, frighteningly so. Marx erred on this score: it will take more than technological stagnation to terminate this system of social relations. As new issues challenge the validity of the entire system, the political and ecological domains will become all the more important. Alternatively, we are faced with the prospect that capitalism may pull down the entire world and leave behind little more than ashes and ruin—achieving, in short, the "capitalist barbarism" of which Rosa Luxemburg warned in her "Junius" essay.

Marxism was the most comprehensive and coherent effort to produce a systematic form of socialism, emphasizing the material as well as the subjective historical preconditions of a new society. We owe much to Marx's attempt to provide us with a coherent and stimulating analysis of the commodity and commodity relations, to an activist philosophy, a systematic social theory, an objectively grounded or "scientific" concept of historical development, and a flexible political strategy. Marxist political ideas were eminently relevant to the needs of a terribly disoriented proletariat and to the particular oppressions that the industrial bourgeoisie inflicted upon it in England in the 1840s, somewhat later in France, Italy, and Germany, and very presciently in Russia in the last decade of Marx's life. Until the rise of the populist movement in Russia (most famously, the *Narodnaya Volya*), Marx expected the emerging proletariat to become the great majority of the population in Europe and North America, and to inevitably engage in revolutionary class war as a result of capitalist exploitation and immiseration. And especially between 1917 and 1939, long after Marx's death, Europe was indeed beleaguered by a mounting class war that reached the point of outright workers' insurrections. In 1917, owing to an extraordinary confluence of circumstances—particularly with the outbreak of the First World War, which rendered several quasi-feudal European social systems terribly unstable—Lenin and the Bolsheviks tried to use (but greatly altered) Marx's writings in order to take power in an economically backward empire, whose size spanned eleven time zones across Europe and Asia.[4]

---

4 I use the word *extraordinary* because, by Marxist standards, Europe was still objectively unprepared for a socialist revolution in 1914. Much of the continent, in fact, had yet to be colonized by the capitalist market or bourgeois social relations. The proletariat—still a very conspicuous minority of the population in a sea of peasants and small producers—had yet to mature as a class into a significant force. Despite the opprobrium that has been heaped on Plekhanov, Kautsky, Bernstein et al., they had a better understanding of the failure of Marxist socialism to embed itself in proletarian consciousness than did Lenin. Luxemburg, in any case, straddled the so-called "social-patriotic" and

But for the most part, as we have seen, Marxism's economic insights belonged to an era of emerging factory capitalism in the nineteenth century. Brilliant as a theory of the material preconditions for socialism, it did not address the ecological, civic, and subjective forces or the efficient causes that could impel humanity into a movement for revolutionary social change. On the contrary, for nearly a century, Marxism stagnated theoretically. Its theorists were often puzzled by developments that had passed it by and, since the 1960s, have mechanically appended environmentalist and feminist ideas to its formulaic *ouvrierist* outlook. By the same token, anarchism represents, even in its authentic form, a highly individualistic outlook that fosters a radically unfettered lifestyle, often as a substitute for mass action.

In fact, anarchism represents the most extreme formulation of liberalism's ideology of unfettered autonomy, culminating in a celebration of heroic acts of defiance of the state. Anarchism's mythos of self-regulation (*auto nomos*)—the radical assertion of the individual over or even against society and the personalistic absence of responsibility for the collective welfare—leads to a radical affirmation of the all-powerful will so central to Nietzsche's ideological peregrinations. Some self-professed anarchists have even denounced mass social action as futile and alien to their private concerns and made a fetish of what the Spanish anarchists called *grupismo*, a

---

"internationalist" camps in her image of a Marxist party's function, in contrast to Lenin, her principal opponent in the so-called "organizational question" in the Left of the wartime socialists, who was prepared to establish a "proletarian dictatorship" under all and any circumstances. The First World War was by no means inevitable, and it generated democratic and nationalist revolutions rather than proletarian ones. (Russia, in this respect, was no more a "workers' state" under Bolshevik rule than were the Hungarian and Bavarian "soviet" republics.) Not until 1939 was Europe placed in a position where a world war was inevitable. The revolutionary Left (to which I belonged at the time) frankly erred profoundly when it took a so-called "internationalist" position and refused to support the Allies (their imperialist pathologies notwithstanding) against the vanguard of world fascism, the Third Reich.

small-group mode of action that is highly personal rather than social.

Anarchism has often been confused with revolutionary syndicalism, a highly structured and well-developed mass form of libertarian trade unionism that, unlike anarchism, was long committed to democratic procedures,[5] to discipline in action, and to organized, long-range revolutionary practice to eliminate capitalism. Its affinity with anarchism stems from its strong libertarian bias, but bitter antagonisms between anarchists and syndicalists have a long history in nearly every country in Western Europe and North America, as witness the tensions between the Spanish CNT and the anarchist groups associated with *Tierra y Libertad* early in the twentieth century, between the revolutionary syndicalist and anarchist groups in Russia during the 1917 revolution, and between the IWW in the United States and Sweden, to cite the more illustrative cases in the history of the libertarian labor movement.

Revolutionary syndicalism's destiny has been tied in varying degrees to a pathology called *ouvrierisme*, or "workerism," and whatever philosophy, theory of history, or political economy it possesses has been borrowed, often piecemeal and indirectly, from Marx. Indeed, Georges Sorel and many other professed revolutionary syndicalists in the early twentieth century expressly regarded themselves as Marxists and even more expressly eschewed anarchism. Moreover, revolutionary syndicalism lacks a strategy for social change beyond the general strike; revolutionary uprisings such as the famous October and November general strikes in Russia during 1905 proved to be stirring but ultimately ineffectual. Indeed, as invaluable as the general strike may be as a prelude to direct confrontation with the state, they decidedly do not have the mystical capacity that

---

5 Kropotkin, for example, rejected democratic decision-making procedures: "Majority rule is as defective as any other kind of rule," he asserted. See Peter Kropotkin, "Anarchist Communism: Its Basis and Principles," in *Kropotkin's Revolutionary Pamphlets*, edited by Roger N. Baldwin (1927; reprinted by New York: Dover, 1970), 68.

revolutionary syndicalists assigned to them as means for social change. Their limitations are striking evidence that, as episodic forms of direct action, general strikes are not equatable with revolution nor even with profound social changes, which presuppose a mass movement and require years of gestation and a clear sense of direction. Indeed, revolutionary syndicalism exudes a typical *ouvrierist* anti-intellectualism that disdains attempts to formulate a purposive revolutionary direction and has a reverence for proletarian "spontaneity," which, at times, has led it into highly self-destructive situations. Lacking the means for an analysis of their situation, the Spanish syndicalists (and anarchists) revealed only a minimal capacity to understand the situation in which they found themselves after their victory over Franco's forces in the summer of 1936 and no capacity to take "the next step" to institutionalize a workers and peasants' form of government.

What these observations add up to is that Marxists, revolutionary syndicalists, and authentic anarchists all have a fallacious understanding of politics, which should be conceived as the civic arena and the institutions by which people democratically and directly manage their community affairs. Indeed, the Left has repeatedly mistaken statecraft for politics by its persistent failure to understand that the two are not only radically different but exist in radical tension—in fact, opposition—to each other.[6] As I have written elsewhere, historically, politics did not emerge from the state—an apparatus whose professional machinery is designed to dominate and facilitate the exploitation of the citizenry in the interests of a privileged class. Rather, politics, almost by definition, is the active engagement of free citizens in the handling of their municipal affairs and in their defense of its freedom. One can almost say that politics is the "embodiment" of what the French revolutionaries of the 1790s called *civicisme*. Quite properly, in fact, the word *politics* itself

---

6   I have made the distinction between politics and statecraft in, for example, Murray Bookchin, *From Urbanization to Cities: Toward a New Politics of Citizenship* (1987; reprinted by London: Cassell, 1992), 41–3, 59–61.

contains the Greek word for "city" or *polis*, and its use in classical Athens, together with democracy, connoted the direct governing of the city by its citizens. Centuries of civic degradation, marked particularly by the formation of classes, were necessary to produce the state and its corrosive absorption of the political realm.

A defining feature of the Left is precisely the Marxist, anarchist, and revolutionary syndicalist belief that no distinction exists, in principle, between the political realm and the statist realm. By emphasizing the nation-state—including a "workers' state"—as the locus of economic as well as political power, Marx (as well as libertarians) notoriously failed to demonstrate how workers could fully and directly control such a state without the mediation of an empowered bureaucracy and essentially statist (or equivalently, in the case of libertarians, governmental) institutions. As a result, the Marxists unavoidably saw the political realm, which it designated a workers' state, as a repressive entity, ostensibly based on the interests of a single class: the proletariat.

Revolutionary syndicalism, for its part, emphasized factory control by workers' committees and confederal economic councils as the locus of social authority, thereby simply bypassing any popular institutions that existed outside the economy. Oddly, this was economic determinism with a vengeance, which, tested by the experiences of the Spanish revolution of 1936, proved completely ineffectual. A vast domain of real governmental power, from military affairs to the administration of justice, fell to the Stalinists and the liberals of Spain, who used their authority to subvert the libertarian movement and with it, the revolutionary achievements of the syndicalist workers in July 1936, or what was dourly called by one novelist "The Brief Summer of Spanish Anarchism."

As for anarchism, Bakunin expressed the typical view of its adherents in 1871 when he wrote that the new social order could be created "only through the development and organization of the nonpolitical or antipolitical social power of the working class in city and country," thereby rejecting with characteristic inconsistency the very municipal politics that he sanctioned in Italy around the same year. Accordingly, anarchists have long regarded every government as a state and condemned it—a view that is a recipe for the elimination of any organized social life whatever. While the state is the instrument by which an oppressive and exploitative class regulates and coercively controls the behavior of an exploited class by a ruling class, a government—or better still, a polity—is an ensemble of institutions designed to deal with the problems of consociational life in an orderly and hopefully fair manner. Every institutionalized association that constitutes a system for handling public affairs—with or without the presence of a state—is necessarily a government. By contrast, every state, although necessarily a form of government, is a force for class repression and control. Annoying as it must seem to Marxists and anarchists alike, the cry for a constitution, for a responsible and a responsive government, and even for law or *nomos* has been clearly articulated—and committed to print!—by the oppressed for centuries against the capricious rule exercised by monarchs, nobles, and bureaucrats. The libertarian opposition to law, not to speak of government as such, has been as silly as the image of a snake swallowing its tail. What remains in the end is nothing but a retinal afterimage that has no existential reality.

The issues raised in the preceding pages are of more than academic interest. As we enter the twenty-first century, social radicals need a socialism—libertarian and revolutionary—that is neither an extension of the peasant-craft "associationism" that lies at the core of anarchism nor the proletarianism that lies at the core of revolutionary syndicalism and Marxism. However fashionable the traditional ideologies (particularly anarchism) may be among young people today, a truly progressive socialism that is informed by libertarian as well as Marxian ideas but transcends these older ideologies must provide intellectual leadership. For political radicals today to simply resuscitate Marxism, anarchism, or revolutionary syndicalism and endow them with ideological immortality would be obstructive to the development of a relevant radical movement. A new and comprehensive revolutionary outlook is needed, one that is capable of systematically addressing the generalized issues that may potentially bring most of society into opposition to an ever-evolving and changing capitalist system.

The clash between a predatory society based on indefinite expansion and nonhuman nature has given rise to an ensemble of ideas that has emerged as the explication of the present social crisis and meaningful radical change. Social ecology, a coherent vision of social development that intertwines the mutual impact of hierarchy and class on the civilizing of humanity, has for decades argued that we must reorder social relations so that humanity can live in a protective balance with the natural world.[7]

Contrary to the simplistic ideology of "eco-anarchism," social ecology maintains that an ecologically oriented society can be progressive rather than regressive, placing a strong emphasis not on primitivism, austerity, and denial but on material pleasure and ease. If a society is to be capable of making life not only vastly enjoyable for its members but also leisurely enough that they can engage in the intellectual and cultural self-cultivation that is necessary for creating civilization and a vibrant political life, it must not denigrate technics and science but bring them into accord with visions of human happiness and leisure. Social ecology is an ecology not of hunger and material deprivation but of plenty; it seeks the creation of a rational society in which waste, indeed excess, will be controlled by a new system of values; and when or if shortages arise as a result of irrational behavior, popular assemblies will establish rational standards of consumption by democratic processes. In short, social ecology favors management, plans, and regulations formulated democratically by popular assemblies, not

---

7 Several years ago, while I still identified myself as an anarchist, I attempted to formulate a distinction between "social" and "lifestyle" anarchism, and I wrote an article that identified Communalism as "the democratic dimension of anarchism" (see *Left Green Perspectives*, no. 31, October 1994). I no longer believe that Communalism is a mere "dimension" of anarchism, democratic or otherwise; rather, it is a distinct ideology with a revolutionary tradition that has yet to be explored.

freewheeling forms of behavior that have their origin in individual eccentricities.

It is my contention that Communalism is the overarching political category most suitable to encompass the fully thought-out and systematic views of social ecology, including libertarian municipalism and dialectical naturalism. As an ideology, Communalism draws on the best of the older Left ideologies—Marxism and anarchism, more properly the libertarian socialist tradition—while offering a wider and more relevant scope for our time. From Marxism, it draws the basic project of formulating a rationally systematic and coherent socialism that integrates philosophy, history, economics, and politics. Avowedly dialectical, it attempts to infuse theory with practice. From anarchism, it draws its commitment to antistatism and confederalism, as well as its recognition that hierarchy is a basic problem that can be overcome only by a libertarian socialist society.[8]

The choice of the term *Communalism* to encompass the philosophical, historical, political, and organizational components of a socialism for the twenty-first century has not been an offhanded one. The word originated in the Paris Commune of 1871, when the armed people of the French capital raised barricades not only to defend the city council of Paris and its administrative substructures but also to create a nationwide confederation of cities and towns to replace the republican nation-state. Communalism as an ideology is not sullied by the individualism and the often explicit antirationalism of anarchism; nor does it carry the historical burden

---

8   To be sure, these points undergo modification in Communalism: for example, Marxism's historical materialism, explaining the rise of class societies, is expanded by social ecology's explanation of the anthropological and historical rise of hierarchy. Marxian dialectical materialism, in turn, is transcended by dialectical naturalism; and the anarcho-communist notion of a very loose "federation of autonomous communes" is replaced with a confederation from which its components, functioning in a democratic manner through citizens' assemblies, may withdraw only with the approval of the confederation as a whole.

of Marxism's authoritarianism as embodied in Bolshevism. It does not focus on the factory as its principal social arena or on the industrial proletariat as its main historical agent; and it does not reduce the free community of the future to a fanciful medieval village. Its most important goal is clearly spelled out in a conventional dictionary definition: Communalism, according to the American Heritage Dictionary of the English Language, is "a theory or system of government in which virtually autonomous local communities are loosely bound in a federation."[9]

Communalism seeks to recapture the meaning of politics in its broadest, most emancipatory sense, indeed, to fulfill the historic potential of the municipality as the developmental arena of mind and discourse. It conceptualizes the municipality, potentially at least, as a transformative development beyond organic evolution into the domain of social evolution. The city is the domain where the archaic blood-tie that was once limited to the unification of families and tribes, to the exclusion of outsiders, was—juridically, at least—dissolved. It became the domain where hierarchies based on parochial and sociobiological attributes of kinship, gender, and age could be eliminated and replaced by a free society based on a shared common humanity. Potentially, it remains the domain where the once-feared stranger can be fully absorbed into the community—initially as a protected resident of a common territory and eventually as a citizen, engaged in making policy decisions in the public arena. It is above all the domain where institutions and values have their roots not in zoology but in civil human activity.

Looking beyond these historical functions, the municipality constitutes the only domain for an association based on the free exchange of ideas and a creative endeavor to bring the capacities of consciousness to the service of freedom. It is the domain where a mere

---

9   What is so surprising about this minimalist dictionary definition is its overall accuracy: I would take issue only with its formulations "virtually autonomous" and "loosely bound," which suggest a parochial and particularistic, even irresponsible relationship of the components of a confederation to the whole.

animalistic adaptation to an existing and pregiven environment can be radically supplanted by proactive, rational intervention into the world—indeed, a world yet to be made and molded by reason—with a view toward ending the environmental, social, and political insults to which humanity and the biosphere have been subjected by classes and hierarchies. Freed of domination as well as material exploitation—indeed, re-created as a rational arena for human creativity in all spheres of life—the municipality becomes the ethical space for the good life. Communalism is thus no contrived product of mere fancy: it expresses an abiding concept and practice of political life, formed by a dialectic of social development and reason.

As an explicitly political body of ideas, Communalism seeks to recover and advance the development of the city in a form that accords with its greatest potentialities and historical traditions. This is not to say that Communalism accepts the municipality as it is today. Quite to the contrary, the modern municipality is infused with many statist features and often functions as an agent of the bourgeois nation-state. Today, when the nation-state still seems supreme, the rights that modern municipalities possess cannot be dismissed as the epiphenomena of more basic economic relations. Indeed, to a great degree, they are the hard-won gains of commoners, who long defended them against assaults by ruling classes over the course of history—even against the bourgeoisie itself.

The concrete political dimension of Communalism is known as libertarian municipalism.[10] In its libertarian municipalist program, Communalism resolutely seeks to eliminate statist municipal

---

10   My extensive writings on libertarian municipalism date back to the early 1970s, with "Spring Offensives and Summer Vacations," *Anarchos*, no. 4, 1972. The more significant works include *From Urbanization to Cities*, 1987, reprinted by London: Cassell, 1992; "Theses on Libertarian Municipalism," *Our Generation* [Montreal], vol. 16, nos. 3–4, Spring/Summer 1985; "Radical Politics in an Era of Advanced Capitalism," *Green Perspectives*, no. 18, Nov. 1989; "The Meaning of Confederalism," *Green Perspectives*, no. 20, November 1990; "Libertarian Municipalism: An Overview," *Green Perspectives*, no. 24, October 1991; and *The Limits of the City*, New York: Harper Colophon, 1974.

structures and replace them with the institutions of a libertarian polity. It seeks to radically restructure cities' governing institutions into popular democratic assemblies based on neighborhoods, towns, and villages. In these popular assemblies, citizens—including the middle classes as well as the working classes—deal with community affairs on a face-to-face basis, making policy decisions in a direct democracy and giving reality to the ideal of a humanistic, rational society.

Minimally, if we are to have the kind of free social life to which we aspire, democracy should be our form of a shared political life. To address problems and issues that transcend the boundaries of a single municipality, in turn, the democratized municipalities should join together to form a broader confederation. These assemblies and confederations, by their very existence, could then challenge the legitimacy of the state and statist forms of power. They could expressly be aimed at replacing state power and statecraft with popular power and a socially rational transformative politics. And they would become arenas where class conflicts could be played out and where classes could be eliminated.

Libertarian municipalists do not delude themselves that the state will view with equanimity their attempts to replace professionalized power with popular power. They harbor no illusions that the ruling classes will indifferently allow a Communalist movement to demand rights that infringe on the state's sovereignty over towns and cities. Historically, regions, localities, and above all towns and cities have desperately struggled to reclaim their local sovereignty from the state (albeit not always for high-minded purposes). Communalists' attempt to restore the powers of towns and cities and to knit them together into confederations can be expected to evoke increasing resistance from national institutions. That the new popular-assemblyist municipal confederations will embody a dual power against the state that becomes a source of growing political tension is obvious. Either a Communalist movement will be radicalized by this tension and will resolutely face all its consequences or it will surely sink into a morass of compromises that absorb it back into the social order that it once sought to change. How the movement meets this challenge is a clear measure of its seriousness in seeking to change the existing political system and the social consciousness it develops as a source of public education and leadership.

Communalism constitutes a critique of hierarchical and capitalist society as a whole. It seeks to alter not only the political life of society but also its economic life. On this score, its aim is not to nationalize the economy or retain private ownership of the means of production but to municipalize the economy. It seeks to integrate the means of production into the existential life of the municipality such that every productive enterprise falls under the purview of the local assembly, which decides how it will function to meet the interests of the community as a whole. The separation between life and work, so prevalent in the modern capitalist economy, must be overcome so that citizens' desires and needs, the artful challenges of creation in the course of production, and role of production in fashioning thought and self-definition are not lost. "Humanity makes itself," to cite the title of V. Gordon Childe's book on the urban revolution at the end of the Neolithic age and the rise of cities, and it does so not only intellectually and aesthetically but by expanding human needs as well as the productive methods for satisfying them. We discover ourselves—our potentialities and their actualization—through creative and useful work that not only transforms the natural world but leads to our self-formation and self-definition.

We must also avoid the parochialism and ultimately the desires for proprietorship that have afflicted so many self-managed enterprises, such as the "collectives" in the Russian and Spanish revolutions. Not enough has been written about the drift among many "socialistic" self-managed enterprises, even under the red and red-and-black flags, respectively, of revolutionary Russia and revolutionary Spain, toward forms of collective capitalism that ultimately led many of these concerns to compete with one another for raw materials and markets.[11]

---

11 For one such discussion, see Murray Bookchin, "The Ghost of Anarchosyndicalism,"*Anarchist Studies*, vol. 1, no. 1, Spring 1993.

Most importantly, in Communalist political life, workers of different occupations would take their seats in popular assemblies not as workers—printers, plumbers, foundry workers, and the like, with special occupational interests to advance—but as citizens, whose overriding concern should be the general interest of the society in which they live. Citizens should be freed of their particularistic identity as workers, specialists, and individuals concerned primarily with their own particularistic interests. Municipal life should become a school for the formation of citizens, both by absorbing new citizens and by educating the young, while the assemblies themselves should function not only as permanent decision-making institutions but as arenas for educating the people in handling complex civic and regional affairs.[12]

In a Communalist way of life, conventional economics, with its focus on prices and scarce resources, would be replaced by ethics, with its concern for human needs and the good life. Human solidarity—or *philia*, as the Greeks called it—would replace material gain and egotism. Municipal assemblies would become not only vital arenas for civic life and decision-making but centers where the shadowy world of economic logistics, properly coordinated production, and civic operations would be demystified and opened to the scrutiny and participation of the citizenry as a whole. The emergence of the new citizen would mark a transcendence of the particularistic class being of traditional socialism and the formation of the "new man," which the Russian revolutionaries hoped they

---

12   One of the great tragedies of the Russian Revolution of 1917 and the Spanish Revolution of 1936 was the failure of the masses to acquire more than the scantest knowledge of social logistics and the complex interlinkages involved in providing for the necessities of life in a modern society. Inasmuch as those who had the expertise involved in managing productive enterprises and in making cities functional were supporters of the old regime, workers were in fact unable to actually take over the full control of factories. They were obliged instead to depend on "bourgeois specialists" to operate them, individuals who steadily made them the victims of a technocratic elite.

could eventually achieve. Humanity would now be able to rise to the universal state of consciousness and rationality that the great utopians of the nineteenth century and the Marxists hoped their efforts would create, opening the way to humanity's fulfillment as a species that embodies reason rather than material interest and that affords material postscarcity rather than an austere harmony enforced by a morality of scarcity and material deprivation.[13]

Classical Athenian democracy of the fifth century BCE, the source of the Western democratic tradition, was based on face-to-face decision-making in communal assemblies of the people and confederations of those municipal assemblies. For more than two millennia, the political writings of Aristotle recurrently served to heighten our awareness of the city as the arena for the fulfillment of human potentialities for reason, self-consciousness, and the good life. Appropriately, Aristotle traced the emergence of the polis from the family or *oikos*, that is, the realm of necessity, where human beings satisfied their basically animalistic needs and where authority rested with the eldest male. But the association of several families, he observed, "aim[ed] at something more than the supply of daily needs";[14] this aim initiated the earliest political formation, the village. Aristotle famously described man (by which he meant the adult Greek male)[15] as a "political animal" (*politikon zoon*), who

---

13 I have previously discussed this transformation of workers from mere class beings into citizens, among other places, in *From Urbanization to Cities*, 1987, reprinted by London: Cassell, 1995; and in "Workers and the Peace Movement," 1983, published in *The Modern Crisis*, Montreal: Black Rose Books, 1987.

14 Aristotle, *Politics* (1252 [b] 16), trans. Benjamin Jowett, in *The Complete Works of Aristotle*, Revised Oxford Translation, ed. J. Barnes, Princeton, NJ: Princeton University Press, 1984, vol. 2, 1987.

15 As a libertarian ideal for the future of humanity and a genuine domain of freedom, the Athenian polis falls far short of the city's ultimate promise. Its population included slaves, subordinated women, and franchiseless resident aliens. Only a minority of male citizens possessed civic rights, and they ran the city without consulting a larger population. Materially, the stability of the polis

22

presided over family members not only to meet their material needs but as the material precondition for his participation in political life, in which discourse and reason replaced mindless deeds, custom, and violence. Thus, "when several villages are united in a single complete community (*koinonan*), large enough to be nearly or quite self-sufficing," he continued, "the *polis* comes into existence, originating in the bare needs of life, and continuing in existence for the sake of a good life."[16]

For Aristotle, and we may assume also for the ancient Athenians, the municipality's proper functions were thus not strictly instrumental or even economic. As the locale of human consociation, the municipality, and the social and political arrangements that people living there constructed, was humanity's *telos*, the arena par excellence where human beings, over the course of history, could actualize their potentiality for reason, self-consciousness, and creativity. Thus, for the ancient Athenians, politics denoted not only the handling of the practical affairs of a polity but civic activities that were charged with moral obligation to one's community. All citizens of a city were expected to participate in civic activities as ethical beings.

Examples of municipal democracy were not limited to ancient Athens. Quite to the contrary, long before class differentiations gave rise to the state, many relatively secular towns produced the earliest institutional structures of local democracy. Assemblies of the people may have existed in ancient Sumer at the very beginning of the so-called "urban revolution" some seven or eight thousand years ago. They clearly appeared among the Greeks, and until the defeat of the Gracchus brothers, they were popular centers of power in republican

---

depended upon the labor of its noncitizens. These are among the several monumental failings that later municipalities would have to correct. The polis is significant, however, not as an example of an emancipated community but for the successful functioning of its free institutions.

16   Aristotle, *Politics* (1252 [b] 29–30), trans. Jowett; emphasis added. The words from the original Greek text may be found in the Loeb Classical Library edition: Aristotle, *Politics*, trans. H. Rackham (Cambridge, MA: Harvard University Press, 1972).

Rome. They were nearly ubiquitous in the medieval towns of Europe and even in Russia, notably in Novgorod and Pskov, which, for a time, were among the most democratic cities in the Slavic world. The assembly, it should be emphasized, began to approximate its truly modern form in the neighborhood Parisian sections of 1793, when they became the authentic motive forces of the Great Revolution and conscious agents for the making of a new body politic. That they were never given the consideration they deserve in the literature on democracy, particularly democratic Marxist tendencies and revolutionary syndicalists, is dramatic evidence of the flaws that existed in the revolutionary tradition.

These democratic municipal institutions normally existed in combative tension with grasping monarchs, feudal lords, wealthy families, and freebooting invaders until they were crushed, frequently in bloody struggles. It cannot be emphasized too strongly that every great revolution in modern history had a civic dimension that has been smothered in radical histories by an emphasis on class antagonisms, however important these antagonisms have been. Thus, it is unthinkable that the English Revolution of the 1640s can be understood without singling out London as its terrain; or, by the same token, any discussions of the various French Revolutions without focusing on Paris, or the Russian Revolutions without dwelling on Petrograd, or the Spanish Revolution of 1936 without citing Barcelona as its most advanced social center. This centrality of the city is not a mere geographic fact; it is, above all, a profoundly political one, which involved the ways in which revolutionary masses aggregated and debated, the civic traditions that nourished them, and the environment that fostered their revolutionary views.

Libertarian municipalism is an integral part of the Communalist framework, indeed its praxis, just as Communalism as a systematic body of revolutionary thought is meaningless without libertarian municipalism. The differences between Communalism and authentic or "pure" anarchism, let alone Marxism, are much too great to be spanned by a prefix such as anarcho-, social, neo-, or even libertarian. Any attempt to reduce Communalism to a mere variant of anarchism would be to deny the integrity of both ideas; indeed, to ignore their conflicting concepts of democracy, organization, elections, government, and the like. Gustave Lefrançais, the Paris Communard who may have coined this political term, adamantly declared that he was "a Communalist, not an anarchist."[17]

Above all, Communalism is engaged with the problem of power.[18] In marked contrast to the various kinds of communitarian enterprises favored by many self-designated anarchists, such as "people's" garages, print shops, food co-ops, and backyard gardens, adherents of Communalism mobilize themselves to electorally engage in a potentially important center of power—the municipal council—and try to compel it to create legislatively potent neighborhood assemblies. These assemblies, it should be emphasized, would make every effort to delegitimate and depose the statist organs that currently control their villages, towns, or cities and thereafter act as the

---

17   Lefrançais is quoted in Peter Kropotkin, *Memoirs of a Revolutionist*, New York: Horizon Press, 1968, 393. I too would be obliged today to make the same statement. In the late 1950s, when anarchism in the United States was a barely discernible presence, it seemed like a sufficiently clear field in which I could develop social ecology, as well as the philosophical and political ideas that would eventually become dialectical naturalism and libertarian municipalism. I well knew that these views were not consistent with traditional anarchist ideas, least of all postscarcity, which implied that a modern libertarian society rested on advanced material preconditions. Today, I find that anarchism remains the very simplistic individualistic and antirationalist psychology it has always been. My attempt to retain anarchism under the name of "social anarchism" has largely been a failure, and I now find that the term I have used to denote my views must be replaced with Communalism, which coherently integrates and goes beyond the most viable features of the anarchist and Marxist traditions. Recent attempts to use the word *anarchism* as a leveler to minimize the abundant and contradictory differences that are grouped under that term and even celebrate its openness to "differences" make it a diffuse catch-all for tendencies that properly should be in sharp conflict with one another.

18   For a discussion of the very real problems created by anarchists' disdain for power during the 1936 Spanish Revolution, see the article, "Anarchism and Power in the Spanish Revolution."

real engines in the exercise of power. Once a number of municipalities are democratized along Communalist lines, they would methodically confederate into municipal leagues and challenge the role of the nation-state and, through popular assemblies and confederal councils, try to acquire control over economic and political life.

Finally, Communalism, in contrast to anarchism, decidedly calls for decision-making by majority voting as the only equitable way for a large number of people to make decisions. Authentic anarchists claim that this principle—the "rule" of the minority by the majority—is authoritarian and propose instead to make decisions by consensus. Consensus, in which single individuals can veto majority decisions, threatens to abolish society as such. A free society is not one in which its members, like Homer's lotus-eaters, live in a state of bliss without memory, temptation, or knowledge. Like it or not, humanity has eaten of the fruit of knowledge, and its memories are laden with history and experience. In a lived mode of freedom—contrary to mere café chatter—the rights of minorities to express their dissenting views will always be protected as fully as the rights of majorities. Any abridgements of those rights would be instantly corrected by the community—hopefully gently, but if unavoidable, forcefully—lest social life collapse into sheer chaos. Indeed, the views of a minority would be treasured as a potential source of new insights and nascent truths that, if abridged, would deny society the sources of creativity and developmental advances— for new ideas generally emerge from inspired minorities that gradually gain the centrality they deserve at a given time and place—until, again, they too are challenged as the conventional wisdom of a period that is beginning to pass away and requires new (minority) views to replace frozen orthodoxies.

It remains to ask, How are we to achieve this rational society? One anarchist writer would have it that the good society (or a true "natural" disposition of affairs, including a "natural man") exists beneath the oppressive burdens of civilization like fertile soil beneath the snow. It follows from this mentality that all we are obliged to do to achieve the good society is to somehow eliminate the snow, which is to say capitalism, nation-states, churches, conventional schools, and other almost endless types of institutions that perversely embody domination in one form or another. Presumably, an anarchist society—once state, governmental, and cultural institutions are merely removed—would emerge intact, ready to function and thrive as a free society. Such a "society," if one can even call it such, would not require that we proactively create it; we would simply let the snow above it melt away. The process of rationally creating a free Communalist society, alas, will require substantially more thought and work than embracing a mystified concept of aboriginal innocence and bliss.

A Communalist society should rest, above all, on the efforts of a new radical organization to change the world—one that has a new political vocabulary to explain its goals, and a new program and theoretical framework to make those goals coherent. It would, above all, require dedicated individuals who are willing to take on the responsibilities of education and leadership. Unless words are not to become completely mystified and obscure a reality that exists before our very eyes, it should minimally be acknowledged that leadership always exists and does not disappear because it is clouded by euphemisms such as "militants" or, as in Spain, "influential militants." It must also be acknowledged that many individuals in earlier groups, like the CNT, were not just "influential militants" but outright leaders, whose views were given more consideration—and deservedly so!—than those of others because they were based on more experience, knowledge, and wisdom, as well as the psychological traits that were needed to provide effective guidance. A serious libertarian approach to leadership would indeed acknowledge the reality and crucial importance of leaders—all the more to establish the greatly needed formal structures and regulations that can effectively control and modify the activities of leaders and recall them when the membership decides their respect is being misused or when leadership becomes an exercise in the abuse of power.

A libertarian municipalist movement should function, not with the adherence of flippant and tentative members, but with people who have been schooled in the movement's ideas, procedures, and activities. They should, in effect, demonstrate a serious commitment to their organization—an organization whose structure is laid out explicitly in a formal constitution and appropriate bylaws. Without a democratically formulated and approved institutional framework whose members and leaders can be held accountable, clearly articulated standards of responsibility cease to exist. Indeed, it is precisely when a membership is no longer responsible to its constitutional and regulatory provisions that authoritarianism develops and eventually leads to the movement's immolation. Freedom from authoritarianism can best be assured only by the clear, concise, and detailed allocation of power, not by pretensions that power and leadership are forms of "rule" or by libertarian metaphors that conceal their reality. It has been precisely when an organization fails to articulate these regulatory details that the conditions emerge for its degeneration and decay.

Ironically, no stratum has been more insistent in demanding its freedom to exercise its will against regulation than chiefs, monarchs, nobles, and the bourgeoisie; similarly, even well-meaning anarchists have seen individual autonomy as the true expression of freedom from the "artificialities" of civilization. In the realm of true freedom, that is, freedom that has been actualized as the result of consciousness, knowledge, and necessity, to know what we can and cannot do is more cleanly honest and true to reality than to avert the responsibility of knowing the limits of the lived world. As Marx observed more than a century and a half ago, "Men make their own history, but they do not make it just as they please."

The need for the international Left to advance courageously beyond a Marxist, anarchist, syndicalist, or vague socialist framework toward a Communalist framework is particularly compelling today. Rarely in the history of leftist political ideas have ideologies been so wildly and irresponsibly muddled; rarely has ideology itself been so disparaged; rarely has the cry for "Unity!" on any terms been heard with such desperation. To be sure, the various tendencies that oppose capitalism should indeed unite around efforts to discredit and ultimately efface the market system. To such ends, unity is an invaluable desideratum: a united front of the entire Left is needed in order to counter the entrenched system—indeed, culture—of commodity production and exchange, and to defend the residual rights that the masses have won in earlier struggles against oppressive governments and social systems.

The urgency of this need, however, does not require movement participants to abandon mutual criticism or to stifle their criticism of the authoritarian traits present in anticapitalist organization. Least of all does it require them to compromise the integrity and identity of their various programs. The vast majority of participants in today's movement are inexperienced young radicals who have come of age in an era of postmodernist relativism. As a consequence, the movement is marked by a chilling eclecticism, in which tentative opinions are chaotically mismarried to ideals that should rest on soundly objective premises.[19] In a milieu where the clear expression of ideas is not valued and terms are inappropriately used, and where argumentation is disparaged as "aggressive" and worse, "divisive," it becomes difficult to formulate ideas in the crucible of debate. Ideas grow and mature best, in fact, not in the silence and controlled humidity of an ideological nursery but in the tumult of dispute and mutual criticism.

Following revolutionary socialist practices of the past, Communalists would try to formulate a minimum program that calls for the satisfaction of immediate concerns, such as improved wages and shelter or adequate park space and transportation. This

---

19   I should note that by objective, I do not refer merely to existential entities and events but also to potentialities that can be rationally conceived, nurtured, and in time actualized into what we would narrowly call realities. If mere substantiality were all that the term *objective* meant, no ideal or promise of freedom would be an objectively valid goal unless it existed under our very noses.

minimum program would aim to satisfy the most elemental needs of the people, to improve their access to the resources that make daily life tolerable. The maximum program, by contrast, would present an image of what human life could be like under libertarian socialism, at least as far as such a society is foreseeable in a world that is continually changing under the impact of seemingly unending industrial revolutions.

Even more, however, Communalists would see their program and practice as a process. Indeed, a transitional program in which each new demand provides the springboard for escalating demands that lead toward more radical and eventually revolutionary demands. One of the most striking examples of a transitional demand was the programmatic call in the late nineteenth century by the Second International for a popular militia to replace a professional army. In still other cases, revolutionary socialists demanded that railroads be publically owned (or, as revolutionary syndicalists might have demanded, be controlled by railroad workers) rather than privately owned and operated. None of these demands were in themselves revolutionary, but they opened pathways, politically, to revolutionary forms of ownership and operation, which, in turn, could be escalated to achieve the movement's maximum program. Others might criticize such step-by-step endeavors as "reformist," but Communalists do not contend that a Communalist society can be legislated into existence. What these demands try to achieve, in the short term, are new rules of engagement between the people and capital—rules that are all the more needed at a time when "direct action" is being confused with protests of mere events whose agenda is set entirely by the ruling classes.

On the whole, Communalism is trying to rescue a realm of public action and discourse that is either disappearing or that is being reduced to often-meaningless engagements with the police, or to street theater that, however artfully, reduces serious issues to simplistic performances that have no instructive influence. By contrast, Communalists try to build lasting organizations and institutions that can play a socially transformative role in the real world. Significantly, Communalists do not hesitate to run candidates in municipal elections who, if elected, would use what real power their offices confer to legislate popular assemblies into existence. These assemblies, in turn, would have the power ultimately to create effective forms of town-meeting government. Inasmuch as the emergence of the city—and city councils—long preceded the emergence of class society, councils based on popular assemblies are not inherently statist organs, and to participate seriously in municipal elections countervails reformist socialist attempts to elect statist delegates by offering the historical libertarian vision of municipal confederations as a practical, combative, and politically credible popular alternative to state power. Indeed, Communalist candidacies, which explicitly denounce parliamentary candidacies as opportunist, keep alive the debate over how libertarian socialism can be achieved—a debate that has been languishing for years.

There should be no self-deception about the opportunities that exist as a means of transforming our irrational society into a rational one. Our choices on how to transform the existing society are still on the table of history and are faced with immense problems. But unless present and future generations are beaten into complete submission by a culture based on queasy calculation as well as by police with tear gas and water cannons, we cannot desist from fighting for what freedoms we have and try to expand them into a free society wherever the opportunity to do so emerges. At any rate, we now know, in the light of all the weaponry and means of ecological destruction that are at hand, that the need for radical change cannot be indefinitely deferred. What is clear is that human beings are much too intelligent not to have a rational society; the most serious question we face is whether they are rational enough to achieve one.

November 2002

2

The Ecological Crisis and the Need to Remake Society

In addressing the sources of our present ecological and social problems, perhaps the most fundamental message that social ecology advances is that the very *idea* of dominating nature stems from the domination of human by human. The primary implication of this most basic message is a call for a politics and even an economics that offer a democratic alternative to the nation-state and the market society. Here I offer a broad sketch of these issues to lay the groundwork for the changes necessary in moving toward a free and ecological society.

First, the most fundamental route to a resolution of our ecological problems is *social* in character. That is to say, if we are faced with the prospect of outright ecological catastrophe, toward which so many knowledgeable people and institutions claim we are headed today, it is because the historic domination of human by human has been extended outward from society into the natural world. Until domination as such is removed from social life and replaced by a truly communitarian, egalitarian, and sharing society, powerful ideological, technological, and systemic forces will be used by the existing society to degrade the environment, indeed the entire biosphere. Hence, more than ever today, it is imperative that we develop the consciousness and the movement to remove domination from society, indeed from our everyday lives—in relationships between the young and the elderly, between women and men, in educational institutions and workplaces, and in our attitude toward the natural world. To permit the poison of domination—and a domineering sensibility—to persist is, at this time, to ignore the most basic roots of our ecological as well as social problems and their sources, which can be traced back to the very inception of our civilization.

Second, and more specifically, the modern market society that we call capitalism and its alter ego, "state socialism," have brought all the historic problems of domination to a head. The consequences of this "grow or die" market economy must inexorably lead to the destruction of the natural basis for complex life forms, including humanity. It is all too common these days, however, to single out either population growth or technology, or both, to blame for the ecological dislocations that beset us. But we cannot single out either of these as "causes" of problems whose most deep-seated roots actually lie in the market economy. Attempts to focus on these alleged "causes" are scandalously deceptive and shift our focus away from the social issues we must resolve.

In the American experience, people only a generation or two removed from my own slashed their way through the vast forests of the West, nearly exterminated millions of bison, plowed fertile grasslands, and laid waste to a vast part of a continent—all using only hand axes, simple plows, horse-drawn vehicles, and simple hand tools. It required no technological revolution to create the present devastation of what had once been a vast and fecund region capable, with rational management, of sustaining both human and nonhuman life. What brought so much ruin to the land was not the technological implements that those earlier generations of Americans used but the insane drive of entrepreneurs to succeed in the bitter struggle of the marketplace, to expand and devour the riches of their competitors lest they be devoured in turn by their rivals. In my own lifetime, millions of small American farmers were driven from their homes not only by natural disasters but by huge agricultural corporations that turned so much of the landscape into a vast industrial system for cultivating food.

Not only has a society based on endless, wasteful growth devastated entire regions, indeed a continent, with only a simple technology, the ecological crisis it has produced is *systemic*—and not a matter of misinformation, spiritual insensitivity, or lack of moral integrity. The present social illness lies not only in the outlook that pervades the present society; it lies above all in the very *structure* and *law of life in the system* itself, in its imperative, which no entrepreneur or corporation can ignore without facing destruction: growth, more growth, and still more growth. Blaming technology for the ecological crisis serves, however unintentionally, to blind us to the ways technology could in fact play a creative role in a rational, ecological society. In such a society, the intelligent use of a sophisticated technology would be direly needed to restore the vast ecological damage that has already been inflicted on the biosphere, much of which will not repair itself without creative human intervention.

Along with technology, population is commonly singled out for blame as an alleged "cause" of the ecological crisis. But population is by no means the overwhelming threat that some disciples of Malthus in today's ecology movements would have us believe. People do not reproduce like the fruit flies that are so often cited as examples of mindless reproductive growth. They are products of culture, as well as biological nature. Given decent living standards, reasonably educated families often have fewer children in order to improve the quality of their lives. Given education, moreover, and a consciousness of gender oppression, women no longer allow themselves to be reduced to mere reproductive factories. Instead, they stake out claims as humans with all the rights to meaningful and creative lives. Ironically, technology has played a major role in eliminating the domestic drudgery that for centuries culturally stupefied women and reduced them to mere servants of men and men's desire to have children—preferably sons, to be sure. In any case, even if population were to decline for an unspecified reason, the large corporations would try to get people to buy more and still more to render economic expansion possible. Failing to attain a large enough domestic consumers market in which to expand, corporate minds would turn to international markets—or to that most lucrative of all markets, the military.

Finally, well-meaning people who regard New Age moralism, psychotherapeutic approaches, or personal lifestyle changes as the key to resolving the present ecological crisis are destined to be tragically disappointed. No matter how much this society paints itself green or orates on the need for an ecological outlook, the way society literally breathes cannot be undone unless it undergoes profound structural changes: namely, by replacing competition with cooperation, and profit-seeking with relationships based on sharing and mutual concern. Given the present market economy, a corporation or entrepreneur who tried to produce goods in accordance with even a minimally decent ecological outlook would rapidly be devoured by a rival in a marketplace whose selective process of competition rewards the most villainous at the expense of the most virtuous. After all, "business is business," as the maxim has it. And business allows no room for people who are restrained by conscience or moral qualms, as the many scandals in the "business community" attest. Attempting to win the "business community" to an ecological sensibility, let alone to ecologically beneficial practices, would be like asking predatory sharks to live on grass or "persuading" lions to lovingly lie down beside lambs.

The fact is that we are confronted by a thoroughly irrational social system, not simply by predatory individuals who can be won over to ecological ideas by moral arguments, psychotherapy, or even the challenges of a troubled public to their products and behavior. It is less that these entrepreneurs control the present system of savage competition and endless growth than it is that the present system of savage competition and growth controls them. The stagnation of New Age ideology today in the United States attests to its tragic failure to "improve" a social system that must be completely replaced if we are to resolve our ecological crisis. One can only commend the individuals who by virtue of their consumption habits, recycling activities, and appeals for a new sensibility undertake public activities to stop ecological degradation. Each surely does his or her part. But it will require a much greater effort—an organized, clearly conscious, and forward-looking political *movement*—to meet the basic challenges posed by our aggressively anti-ecological society.

Yes, we as individuals should change our lifestyles as much as possible, but it is the utmost shortsightedness to believe that that is all, or even primarily, what we have to do. We need to restructure the entire society, even as we engage in lifestyle changes and single-issue struggles against pollution, nuclear power plants, the excessive use of fossil fuels, the destruction of soil, and so forth. We must have a coherent analysis of the deep-seated hierarchical relationships and systems of domination, as well as of class relationships and economic exploitation that degrade people as well as the environment. Here, we must move beyond the insights provided by the Marxists, syndicalists, and even many liberal economists who for years reduced most social antagonisms and problems to class analysis. Class struggle and economic exploitation still exist, and Marxist class analysis reveals inequities about the present social order that are intolerable.

But the Marxian and liberal belief that capitalism has played a "revolutionary role" in destroying traditional communities and that technological advances seeking to "conquer" nature are a precondition for freedom rings terribly hollow today when many of these very advances are being used to make the most formidable weapons and means of surveillance the world has ever seen. Nor could the Marxian socialists of the 1930s have anticipated how successfully capitalism would use its technological prowess to co-opt the working class and even diminish its numbers in relationship to the rest of the population.

Yes, class *struggles* still exist, but they occur farther and farther below the threshold of class war. Workers, as I can attest from my own experience as a foundryman and as an autoworker for General

Motors, do not regard themselves as mindless adjuncts to machines or as factory dwellers or even as "instruments of history," as Marxists might put it. They regard themselves as *living human beings*: as fathers and mothers, as sons and daughters, as people with dreams and visions, as members of communities—not only of trade unions. Living in towns and cities, their eminently human aspirations go well beyond their "historic role" as class agents of "history." They suffer from the pollution of their communities as well as from their factories, and they are as concerned about the welfare of their children, companions, neighbors, and communities as they are about their jobs and wage scales.

The overly economistic focus of traditional socialism and syndicalism has in recent years caused these movements to lag behind emerging ecological issues and visions—as they lagged, I may add, behind feminist concerns, cultural issues, and urban issues, all of which often cut across class lines to include middle-class people, intellectuals, small proprietors, and even some bourgeois. Their failure to confront hierarchy—not only class and domination, not only economic exploitation—has often alienated women from socialism and syndicalism to the extent that they awakened to the ages-old reality that they have been oppressed irrespective of their class status. Similarly, broad community concerns like pollution afflict people *as such*, whatever the class to which they belong. Disasters like the meltdown of the Chernobyl reactor in Ukraine justly panicked everyone exposed to radiation from the plant, not simply workers and peasants.

Indeed, even if we were to achieve a classless society free of economic exploitation, would we readily achieve a rational society? Would women, young people, the infirm, the elderly, people of color, various oppressed ethnic groups—the list is, in fact, enormous—be free of domination? The answer is a categorical *no*—a fact to which women can certainly attest, even within the socialist and syndicalist movements themselves. Without eliminating the ancient hierarchical and domineering structures from which classes and the state actually emerged, we would have made only a part of the changes needed to achieve a rational society. There would still be a historic toxicant in a socialist or syndicalist society—hierarchy—that would continually erode its highest ideals, namely, the achievement of a truly free and ecological society.

Perhaps the most disquieting feature of many radical groups today, particularly socialists who may accept the foregoing observation, is their commitment to at least a minimal *state* that would coordinate and administer a classless and egalitarian society—a nonhierarchical one, no less! One hears this argument from Andre Gorz and many others who, presumably because of the "complexities" of modern society, cannot conceive of the administration of economic affairs without some kind of coercive mechanism, albeit one with a "human face."

This logistical and in some cases frankly authoritarian view of the human condition (as expressed in the writings of Arne Naess, the father of Deep Ecology) reminds one of a dog chasing its tail. Simply because the "tail" is there—a metaphor for economic "complexity" or market systems of distribution—does not mean that the metaphorical "dog" must chase it in circles that lead nowhere. The "tail" we have to worry about can be rationally simplified by reducing or eliminating commercial bureaucracies, needless reliance on goods from abroad that can be produced by recycling at home, and the underutilization of local resources that are now ignored because they are not "competitively" priced: in short, eliminating the vast paraphernalia of goods and services that may be indispensable to profit-making and competition but not to the rational distribution of goods in a cooperative society. The painful reality is that most excuses in radical theory for preserving a "minimal state" stem from the myopic visions of ecosocialists who can accept the present system of production and exchange as it *is* to one degree or another—not as it *should be* in a moral economy. So conceived, production and distribution seem more formidable—with their bureaucratic machinery, irrational division of labor, and "global" nature—than they actually need be. It would take no great wisdom or array of computers to show with even a grain of imagination how the present "global" system of production and distribution can be simplified and still provide a decent standard of living for everyone. Indeed, it took only some five years to rebuild a ruined Germany after the Second World War, far longer than it would require thinking people today to remove the statist and bureaucratic apparatus for administering the global distribution of goods and resources.

What is even more disquieting is the naïve belief that a "minimal state" could indeed remain "minimal." If history has shown anything, it is that the state, far from being only an instrument of a ruling elite, becomes an organism in its own right that grows as unrelentingly as a cancer. Anarchism, in this respect, has exhibited a prescience that discloses the terrifying weakness of the traditional socialist commitment to a state—proletarian, social democratic, or "minimal." To create a state is to institutionalize power in the form of a machine that exists *apart* from the people. It is to professionalize rule and policymaking, to create a distinct interest (be it of bureaucrats, deputies, commissars, legislators, the military, the police, ad nauseam) that, however weak or however well intentioned it may be at first, eventually takes on a corruptive power of its own. When, over the course of history, have states—however "minimal"—*ever* dissolved themselves or constrained their own growth into massive malignancies? When have they *ever* remained "minimal"?

The deterioration of the German Greens—the so-called "non-party party" that, after its acquisition of a place in the Bundestag, has now become a crude political machine—is dramatic evidence that power corrupts with a vengeance. The idealists who helped found the organization and sought to use the Bundestag merely as a "platform" for their radical message have by now either left it in disgust or have themselves become rather unsavory examples of wanton political careerism. One would have to be utterly naïve or simply blind to the lessons of history to ignore the fact that the state, "minimal" or not, absorbs and ultimately digests even its most well-meaning critics once they enter it. It is not that statists use the state to abolish it or "minimalize" its effects; it is, rather, the state that corrupts even the most idealistic antistatists who flirt with it.

Finally, the most disturbing feature of statism—even "minimal statism"—is that it completely undermines a politics based on confederalism. One of the most unfortunate features of traditional socialist history, Marxian and otherwise, is that it emerged in an era of nation-state building. The Jacobin model of a centralized revolutionary state was accepted almost uncritically by nineteenth-century socialists and became an integral part of the revolutionary tradition—a tradition, I may add, that mistakenly associated itself with the nationalistic emphasis of the French Revolution, as seen in the "Marseillaise" and in its adulation of *la patrie*. Marx's view that the French revolution was basically a model for formulating a revolutionary strategy—he mistakenly claimed that its Jacobin form was the most "classical" of the "bourgeois" revolutions—has had a disastrous effect upon the revolutionary tradition. Lenin adapted this vision so completely that the Bolsheviks were rightly considered the "Jacobins" of the Russian socialist movement, and of course, Stalin used techniques such as purges, show trials, and brute force with lethal effects for the socialist project as a whole.

The notion that human freedom can be achieved, much less perpetuated, through a state of *any* kind is monstrously oxymoronic—a contradiction in terms. Attempts to justify the existence of a cancerous phenomenon like the state and the use of statist measures or "statecraft"—so often mistakenly called "politics," which is actually the self-management of the polis—exclude a radically different form of social management, namely, confederalism. In fact, for centuries, democratic forms of confederalism, in which municipalities were coordinated by mandated and recallable deputies who were always under public scrutiny, have competed with statist forms and constituted a challenging alternative to centralization, bureaucratization, and the professionalization of power in the hands of elite bodies. Let me emphasize that confederalism should not be confused with federalism, which is simply a continuation of nation-states in a network of agreements that preserve the prerogatives of policymaking with little if any citizen involvement. Federalism is simply the state writ large, indeed, the further centralization of already centralized states, as in the United States' federal republic, the European Community, and the recently formed Commonwealth of Independent States—all collections of huge continental super-states that even further remove whatever control people have over nation-states.

A confederalist alternative would be based on a network of pol-icymaking popular assemblies with recallable deputies to local and regional confederal councils—councils whose sole function, I must emphasize, would be to adjudicate differences and undertake strictly administrative tasks. One could scarcely advance such a prospect by making use of a state formation of any kind, however minimal. Indeed, to juggle statist and confederal perspectives in a verbal game by distinguishing "minimal" from "maximal" is to confuse the basis for a new politics structured around participatory democracy. Among Greens in the United States, there have already been ten-dencies that absurdly call for "decentralization" and "grassroots democracy" while seeking to run candidates for state and national offices, that is, for statist institutions, *one of whose essential functions is to confine, restrict, and essentially suppress local democratic institu-tions and initiatives.* Indeed, as I have emphasized in other books and essays, when libertarians of all kinds, but particularly anarchists and ecosocialists, engage in confederal municipalist politics and run for municipal public office, they are not merely seeking to remake cities, towns, and villages on the basis of fully democratic confederal networks, they are running *against* the state and parliamentary offices. Hence, to call for a "minimal state," even as a coordinative institution, as Andre Gorz and others have done, is to obscure and countervail any effort to replace the nation-state with a confedera-tion of municipalities.

It is to the credit of early anarchism and, more recently, to the eco-anarchism that lies at the core of social ecology, that it firmly rejects the traditional socialist orientation toward state power and recognizes the corruptive role of participating in parliamentary elections. What is regrettable is that this rejection, so clearly corroborated by the corruption of statist socialists, Greens, and members of other professed radical movements, was not sufficiently nuanced to distinguish activity on the municipal level (which even Mikhail Bakunin regarded as valid) as the basis of politics in the Hellenic sense: that is to say, to distinguish electoral activity on the local level from electoral activity on the provincial and national levels, which really constitute statecraft.

Social ecology, whatever its other value or failings, represents a coherent interpretation of the enormous ecological and social problems we face today. Its philosophy, social theory, and political practice form a vital alternative to the ideological stagnation and tragic failure of the present socialist, syndicalist, and radical projects that were so much in vogue even as recently as the 1960s. As to "alternatives" that offer us New Age or mystical ecological solutions, what could be more naïve than to believe that a society whose very metabolism is based on growth, production for its own sake, hierarchy, classes, domination, and exploitation could be changed simply by moral suasion, individual action, or a primitivism that essentially views technology as a curse and that focuses variously on demographic growth and personal modes of consumption as primary issues? We must get to the heart of the crisis we face and develop a popular politics that will eschew statism at one extreme and New Age privatism at the other. If this goal is dismissed as utopian, I am obliged to question what many radicals today would call "realism."

January 1992

3

A Politics for the Twenty-First Century

It would be helpful to place libertarian municipalism in a broad historical perspective, all the more to understand its revolutionary character in human affairs generally as well as its place in the repertoire of antistatist practices. The commune, the town or city, or more broadly, the municipality, is not merely a "space" created by a given density of human habitations. In terms of its history as a civilizing tendency in humanity's development, the municipality is integrally part of the sweeping process whereby human beings began to dissolve biologically conditioned social relations based on real or fictitious blood ties, with their primordial hostility to "strangers," and slowly replace them by largely social and rational institutions, rights, and duties that increasingly encompassed all residents of an urban space, irrespective of consanguinity and biological facts. The town, city, municipality, or commune (the equivalent word, in Latin countries, for "municipality") was the emerging civic substitute, based on residence and social interests, for the tribal blood group, which had been based on myths of a common ancestry. The municipality, however slowly and incompletely, formed the necessary condition for human association based on rational discourse, material interest, and a secular culture, irrespective of and often in conflict with ancestral roots and blood ties. Indeed, the fact that people can gather in local assemblies, discuss and share creatively in the exchange of ideas without any hostility or suspicion, despite disparate ethnic, linguistic, and national backgrounds, is a grand historic achievement of civilization, one that is the work of centuries involving a painful discarding of primordial definitions of ancestry and the replacement of these archaic definitions by reason, knowledge, and a growing sense of our status as members of a common humanity.

In great part, this humanizing development was the work of the municipality—the increasingly free space in which people, as people, began to see each other realistically, steadily unfettered by archaic notions of biological ties, tribal affiliations, and a mystical, tradition-laden, and parochial identity. I do not contend that this process of civilization, a term that derives from the Latin word for city and citizenship, has been completely achieved. Far from it: without the existence of a rational society, the municipality can easily become a megalopolis, in which community, however secular, is replaced by atomization and an inhuman social scale beyond the comprehension of its citizens—indeed, the space for class, racial, religious, and other irrational conflicts.

But both historically and contemporaneously, citification forms the necessary condition—albeit by no means fully actualized—for the realization of humanity's potentiality to become fully human, rational, and collectivistic, thereby shedding divisions based on presumed blood affiliations and differences, mindless custom, fearful imaginaries, and a nonrational, often intuitional, notion of rights and duties.

Hence, the municipality is the potential arena for realizing the great goal of transforming parochialized human beings into truly universal human beings, a genuine *humanitas*, divested of the darker brutish attributes of the primordial world. The municipality in which all human beings can be citizens, irrespective of their ethnic background and ideological convictions, constitutes the true arena of a libertarian communist society. Metaphorically speaking, it is not only a desideratum for rational human beings, without which a free society is impossible, it is also the future of a rational humanity, the indispensable space for actualizing humanity's potentialities for freedom and self-consciousness.

I do not presume to claim that a confederation of libertarian municipalities—a Commune of communes—has ever existed in the past. Yet, no matter how frequently I disclaim the existence of any historical "models" and "paradigms" for libertarian municipalities, my critics still try to saddle me with the many social defects of Athens, revolutionary New England towns, and the like, as somehow an integral part of my "ideals." I privilege no single city or group of cities—be they classical Athens, the free cities of the medieval world, the town meetings of the American Revolution, the sections of the Great French Revolution, or the anarchosyndicalist collectives that emerged in the Spanish Revolution—as the full actualization, still less the comprehensive "models" or "paradigms," of the libertarian municipalist vision.

Yet significant features—despite various, often unavoidable distortions—existed among all of these municipalities and the federations that they formed. Their value for us lies in the fact that we can learn from all of them about the ways in which they practiced the democratic precepts by which they were guided. And we can incorporate the best of their institutions for our own and future times, study their defects, and gain inspiration from the fact that they did exist and functioned with varying degrees of success for generations, if not centuries.

At present, I think it is important to recognize that when we advance a politics of libertarian municipalism, we are not engaged in discussing a mere tactic or strategy for creating a public sphere. Rather, we are trying to create a new political culture that is not only consistent with anarchist communist goals but that includes real efforts to actualize these goals, fully cognizant of all the difficulties that face us and the revolutionary implications that they hold for us in the years ahead.

Let me note here that the "neighborhood" is not merely the place where people make their homes, rear their children, and purchase many of their goods. Under a more political coloration, so to speak, a neighborhood may well include those vital spaces where people congregate to discuss political as well as social issues. Indeed, it is the extent to which public issues are openly discussed in a city or town that truly defines the neighborhood as an important political and power space.

By this, I do not mean only an assembly, where citizens discuss and gird themselves to fight for specific policies; I also mean the neighborhood as the center of a town, where citizens may gather as a large group to share their views and give public expression to their policies. This was the function of the Athenian agora, for example, and the town squares in the Middle Ages. The spaces for political life may be multiple, but they are generally highly specific and definable, not random or ad hoc.

Such essentially political neighborhoods have often appeared in times of unrest, when sizable numbers of individuals spontaneously occupy spaces for discussion, as in the Hellenic agora. I recall them during my own youth in New York City, in Union Square and Crotona Park, where hundreds and possibly thousands of men and women appeared weekly to informally discuss the issues of the day. Hyde Park in London constituted such a civic space, as did the Palais-Royal in Paris, which was the breeding ground of the Great French Revolution and the Revolution of 1830.

And during the early days of the 1848 revolution in Paris, scores (possibly hundreds) of neighborhood assembly halls existed as clubs and forums and potentially formed the basis for a restoration of the older neighborhood sections of 1793. The best estimates indicate that club membership did not exceed 70,000 out of a total population of about a million residents. Yet, had this club movement been coordinated by an active and politically coherent revolutionary organization, it could have become a formidable, possibly a successful force, during the weeks of crisis that led to the June insurrection of the Parisian workers.

There is no reason, in principle, why such spaces and the people who regularly occupy them cannot become citizens' assemblies as well. Indeed, like certain sections in the Great French Revolution, they may well take a leading role in sparking a revolution and pushing it forward to its logical conclusion.

A problem exists in anarchist communist theory: it fails to acknowledge that a political sphere, distinguishable from the state and potentially libertarian in its possibilities, must be acknowledged and its potentialities for a truly libertarian politics explored. We cannot content ourselves with simplistically dividing civilization into a workaday world of everyday life that is properly social, as I call it, in which we reproduce the conditions of our individual existence at work, in the home, and among our friends, and, of course, the state, which reduces us at best to docile observers of the activities of professionals who administer our civic and national affairs. Between these two worlds is still another world, the realm of the political, where our ancestors in the past, at various times and places historically, exercised varying, sometimes complete control over the commune and the confederation to which it belonged.

It is a lacuna in anarchist communist theory that the political was conflated with the state, thereby effacing a major distinction between a political sphere in which people in varying degrees exercised power, often through direct assemblies, over their civic environment, and the state, in which people had no direct control, often no control at all, over that environment.

If politics is denatured to mean little more than statecraft and the manipulation of people by their so-called "representatives," then a condition that has acquired varying forms of expression in the classical Athenian assembly, popular medieval civic assemblies, town meetings, and the revolutionary sectional assemblies of Paris, is conveniently erased and the multitudinous institutions for managing a municipality become reducible to the behavior of cynical parliamentarians or worse. It is a gross simplification of historical development and the world in which we live to see the political simply as the practice of statecraft. Just as the tribe emerged long before the city, so the city emerged long before the state—indeed, often in opposition to it. Mesopotamian cities, appearing in the land between the Tigris and Euphrates rivers some six thousand years ago, are believed to have been managed by popular assemblies long before they were forced by intercity conflicts to establish state-like institutions and ultimately despotic imperial institutions. It was in these early cities that politics, that is, popular ways of managing the city, were born and may very well have thrived. The state followed later and elaborated itself institutionally, often in bitter opposition to tendencies that tried to restore popular control over civic affairs.

Nor can we afford to ignore the fact that the same conflict also emerged in early Athens and probably other Greek poleis long before the development of the state reached a relatively high degree of completion. One can see the recurrence of similar conflicts in the struggle of the Gracchi brothers and popular assemblies in Rome against the elitist Senate and, repeatedly, in the medieval cities, long before the rise of late medieval aristocracies and the Baroque monarchies of the fifteenth and sixteenth centuries. Kropotkin did not write nonsense when he pointed to the free cities of Europe, marked not by the existence of states but by their absence.

Indeed, let us also acknowledge that the state itself underwent a process of development and differentiation, at times developing no further than a loose, almost minimal system of coercion, at other times extending further into an ever-growing apparatus, and finally, in this century in particular, acquiring totalitarian control over every aspect of human existence—an apparatus that was only too familiar thousands of years ago in Asia and even in Indian America in pre-Columbian times. The classical Athenian state was only partially statist; it constituted a fraternity, often riven by class conflicts, of select citizens who collectively oppressed slaves, women, and even foreign residents. The medieval state was often a much looser state formation than, say, the Roman imperial state, and at various times in history (one thinks of the *comuñeros* in Spain during the sixteenth century and the sections in France during the eighteenth), the state almost completely collapsed and direct democracies based on communalist political principles played a hegemonic role in social affairs.

Libertarian municipalism is concerned with the political sphere, including aspects of basic civic importance, such as the economic. It does not draw strict impenetrable barriers between the two to the point where they are implacably set against each other. Libertarian municipalism calls for the municipalization of the economy and, where material interests between communities overlap, the confederalization of the economy.

Nor are libertarian municipalists indifferent to the many cultural factors that must play a role in the formation of true citizens, indeed, rounded human beings. But at the same time, let us not reduce every cultural desideratum to the social sphere—to create the myth that the municipality can be reduced to a family—and ignore its overlap with the political. The distinctions between them will only be lost in that poststructural homogenization of everything, making their unique identities almost completely meaningless and potentially, in fact, totalitarian.

Thus, the libertarian municipalist arena may be a school for educating its youth and its mature citizens; but what makes it particularly significant, especially at this time, is that it is a sphere of power relations that must be crystallized against capitalism, the marketplace, the forces for ecological destruction, and the state. Indeed, without a movement that keeps this need completely in mind, libertarian municipalism can easily degenerate in this age of academic specialization into another subject in a classroom curriculum.

Finally, libertarian municipalism rests its politics today on the historically preemptive role of the city in relation to the state, and above all on the fact that civic institutions still exist, however distorted they may appear or however captive to the state they may be, institutions that can be enlarged, radicalized, and eventually aimed at the elimination of the state. The city council, however feeble its powers may be, still exists as the remnant of the communes with which it was identified in the past, especially in the Great French Revolution and the Paris Commune of 1871. The possibility of re-creating a sectional democracy still remains, assuming either a legal or extralegal form. We must bear in mind that the French revolutionary sections did not have any prior tradition on which to rest their claims to legitimacy—indeed, they actually emerged from the elitist assemblies or districts of 1789, which the monarchy had created to elect the Parisian deputies to the Estates General—except that they refused to disband after they completed their electoral role and remained as watchdogs over the behavior of the Estates in Versailles.

We, too, are faced with the task of restructuring and expanding the civic democratic institutions that still exist, however vestigial their forms and powers may be; of attempting to base them on old or new popular assemblies—and, to be quite categorical, of creating new legal or, most emphatically, extralegal popular democratic institutions where vestiges of civic democracy do not exist. In doing so, we are direly in need of a movement—indeed, a responsible, well-structured, and programmatically coherent organization—that can provide the educational resources, means of mobilization, and vital ideas for achieving our libertarian communist and municipalist goals.

Our program should be flexible in the special sense that it poses minimum demands that we seek to achieve at once, given the political sophistication of the community in which we function. But such demands would easily degenerate into reformism if they did not escalate into a body of transitional demands that would ultimately lead to our maximum demands for a libertarian communist society.

Nor can we give up our seemingly utopian vision that the great metropolitan areas can be structurally decentralized. Cities on the scale of New York, London, and Paris, not to speak of Mexico City, Buenos Aires, Bombay, and the like, must ultimately be parceled into smaller cities and decentralized to a point where they are once again humanly scaled communities, not huge and incomprehensible urban belts. Libertarian municipalism takes its immediate point of departure from the existing facts of urban life, many of which are beyond the comprehension of its residents. But it always strives to physically as well as politically fragment the great cities until it achieves the great anarchist communist and even Marxian goal of scaling all cities to human dimensions.

Perhaps the most common criticism that both Marxists and anarchists have presented is the claim that modern cities are too huge to be organized around workable popular assemblies. Some critics assume that if we are to have true democracy, everyone from age zero to one hundred, irrespective of health, mental condition, or disposition, must be included in a popular assembly—and that an assembly must be as small as an "affinity group." But in large world cities, these critics suggest, which have several million residents, we would require many thousands of assemblies in order to achieve true democracy. In such cities, such a multiplicity of small assemblies, they argue, would be just too cumbersome and unworkable.

But a large urban population is itself no obstacle to libertarian municipalism. Indeed, based on this kind of calculation—which would count all residents as participating citizens—the forty-eight Parisian sections of 1793 would have been completely dysfunctional, in view of the fact that revolutionary Paris had a total of 500,000 to 600,000 people. If every man, woman, and child, indeed, ever had attended sectional assemblies, and each assembly had had no more than forty people, my arithmetic tells me that about 15,000 assemblies would have been needed to accommodate all the people of revolutionary Paris. Under such circumstances, one wonders how the French Revolution could ever have occurred.

A popular democracy, to begin with, is not premised on the idea that everyone can, will, or even want to attend popular assemblies. Nor should anyone who professes to be an anarchist make participation compulsory, coercing everyone into doing so. Even more significantly, it has rarely happened—indeed, it has never happened, in my knowledge of revolutionary history—that the great majority of people in a particular place, still less everyone, engages in revolution. In the face of insurrection in a revolutionary situation, while unknown militants, aided by a fairly small number of supporters, rise up and overthrow the established order, most people tend to be observers.

Having reviewed carefully the course of almost every major revolution in the Euro-American world, I can say with some knowledge that even in a completely successful revolution, it was always a minority of the people who attended meetings of assemblies that made significant decisions about the fate of their society. The very differentiated political and social consciousness, interests, education, and backgrounds among masses in a capitalist society guarantee that people will be drawn into revolutions in waves, if at all. The foremost, most militant wave, at first, is numerically surprisingly small; it is followed by seeming bystanders who, if an uprising seems to be capable of success, merge with the first wave, and only after the uprising is likely to be successful do the politically less developed waves, in varying degrees, follow it. Even after an uprising is successful, it takes time for a substantial majority of the people to fully participate in the revolutionary process, commonly as crowds in demonstrations, more rarely as participants in revolutionary institutions.

In the English Revolution of the 1640s, for example, it was primarily the Puritan army that raised the most democratic issues, with the support of the Levellers, who formed a very small fraction of the civilian population. The American Revolution was notoriously supported, albeit by no means actively, by only one-third of the colonial population; the Great French Revolution found its principal support in Paris and was carried forward by forty-eight sections, most of which were rooted in assemblies that were poorly attended, except at times when momentous decisions aroused the most revolutionary neighborhoods.

Indeed, what decided the fate of most revolutions was less the amount of support their militants received than the degree of resistance they encountered. What brought Louis XVI and his family back to Paris from Versailles in October 1789 was certainly not all the women of Paris—indeed, only a few thousand made the famous march to Versailles—but the king's own inability to mobilize a sufficiently large and reliable force to resist them. The Russian Revolution of February 1917 in Petrograd, for many historians the "model" of a mass spontaneous revolution (and an uprising far more nuanced than most accounts suggest), succeeded because not even the tsar's personal guard, let alone such formerly reliable supports of the autocracy as the Cossacks, was prepared to defend the monarchy. Indeed, in revolutionary Barcelona in 1936, the resistance to Franco's forces was initiated by only a few thousand anarchosyndicalists with the aid of the Assault Guards, whose discipline, weaponry, and training were indispensable factors in pinning down and ultimately defeating the regular army's uprising.

It is such constellations of forces, in fact, that explain how revolutions actually succeed. They do not triumph because "everyone," or even a majority of the population, actively participates in overthrowing an oppressive regime, but because the armed forces of the old order and the population at-large are no longer willing to defend it against a militant and resolute minority.

Nor is it likely, however desirable it may be, that after a successful insurrection, the great majority of the people or even the oppressed will personally participate in revolutionizing society. Following the success of a revolution, the majority of people tend to withdraw into the localities in which they live, however large or small, where the problems of everyday life have their most visible impact on the masses. These localities may be residential and/or occupational neighborhoods in large cities, the environs of villages and hamlets, or even at some distance from the center of a city or region, fairly dispersed localities in which people live and work.

No—I do not think the large size of modern cities constitutes an insuperable obstacle to the formation of a neighborhood assembly movement. The doors of the neighborhood assemblies should always be open to whoever lives in the neighborhood. Politically less aware individuals may choose not to attend their neighborhood assembly, and they should not be obliged to attend. The assemblies, regardless of their size, will have problems enough without having to deal with indifferent bystanders and passersby. What counts is that the doors of the assemblies remain open for all who wish to attend and participate, for therein lies the true democratic nature of neighborhood assemblies.

Another criticism against libertarian municipalism is that a large crowd, such as numerous citizens at an assembly meeting, may be manipulated by a forceful speaker or faction. This criticism could be directed against any democratic institution, be it a large assembly, a small committee, an ad hoc conference or meeting, or even an "affinity" group. The size of the group is not a factor here—some very abusive tyrannies appear in very small groups, where one or two intimidating figures can completely dominate everyone else.

What the critics might well ask—but seldom do—is how we are to prevent persuasive individuals from making demagogic attempts to control any popular assembly, regardless of size. In my view, the only obstacle to such attempts is the existence of an organized body of revolutionaries—yes, even a faction—that is committed to seeking truth, exercising rationality, and advancing an ethics of public responsibility. Such an organization will be needed, in my view, not only before and during a revolution but also after one, when the constructive problem of creating stable, enduring, and educational democratic institutions becomes the order of the day.

Such an organization will be particularly needed during the period of social reconstruction when attempts are made to put libertarian municipalism into practice. We cannot expect that, because we propose the establishment of neighborhood assemblies, we will always—or perhaps even often—be the majority in the very institutions that we have significantly helped to establish. We must always be prepared, in fact, to be in the minority, until such time as circumstances and social instability make our overall messages plausible to assembly majorities.

Indeed, wherever we establish a popular assembly, with or without legal legitimacy, it will eventually be invaded by competing class interests. Libertarian municipalism, I should emphasize here, is not an attempt to overlook or evade the reality of class conflict; on the contrary, it attempts, among other things, to give due recognition to the class struggle's civic dimension. Modern conflicts between classes have never been confined simply to the factory or workplace; they have also taken a distinctly urban form, as in "Revolutionary Paris," "Red Petrograd," and "Anarchosyndicalist Barcelona." As any study of the great revolutions vividly reveals, the battle between classes has always been a battle not only between different economic strata in society but also within and between neighborhoods.

Moreover, the neighborhood, town, and village also generates searing issues that cut across class lines: between working people (the traditional industrial proletariat, which is now dwindling in numbers in Europe and the United States and is fighting a rearguard battle with capital), middle-class strata (which lack any consciousness of themselves as working people), the vast army of government employees, a huge professional and technical stratum that is not likely to regard itself as a proletariat, and an underclass that is essentially demoralized and helpless.

We cannot ignore the compelling fact that capitalism has changed since the end of the Second World War; that it has transformed the very social fiber of the great majority of people, both attitudinally and occupationally, in Western Europe and the United States; that it will wreak even further changes in the decades that lie ahead, with dazzling rapidity, especially as automation is further developed and as new resources, techniques, and products replace those that seem so dominant today.

No revolutionary movement can ignore the problems that capitalism is likely to generate in the years that lie ahead, especially in terms of capital's profound effects on both society and the environment. The futility of syndicalism today lies in the fact that it is still trying to address the problems generated by the old industrial revolution and in the context of the social setting that gave these problems meaning in the first half of the twentieth century. If we have historically exhausted the syndicalist alternative, it is because the industrial proletariat is everywhere destined, by virtue of technological innovation, to become a small minority of the population. It will not do to try to theoretically fabricate a "proletariat" out of clerical, service, and professional "workers" who, in many if not most cases, will not acquire the class consciousness that identified and gave a historical standing to the authentic proletarian.

But these strata, often among the most exploited and oppressed, can be enlisted to support our anarchist communist ideals on the basis of the larger environment in which they live and the larger issues of their sovereignty in a world that is racing out of control: namely, their neighborhoods, cities, and towns, and the expansion of their democratic rights as free citizens in a world that has reduced them to mere electoral constituents. They can be mobilized to support our anarchist communist ideals because they feel their power to control their own lives is diminishing in the face of centralized state and corporate power. Needless to say, I am not denying that working people have grim economic problems that may pit them against capital, but their quasi-middle-class outlook if not status diminishes their ability to see the ills of capitalism exclusively as an economic system.

Today, we live in an era of permanent industrial revolution in which people tend to respond to the extreme rapidity and vast scope of change with a mysticism that expresses their disempowerment and a privatism that expresses their inability to contend with change. Indeed, capitalism, far from being "advanced," still less "moribund," continues to mature and extend its scope. What it will look like a half century or a century from now is open to the boldest of speculations.

Hence, more than ever, any revolutionary libertarian communist movement must, in my view, recognize the importance of the municipality as the locus of new, indeed, often transclass problems that cannot simply be reduced to the struggle between wage labor and capital. Real problems of environmental deterioration affect everyone in a community; real problems of social and economic inequities affect everyone in a community; real problems of health, education, sanitary conditions, and the nightmare, as Paul Goodman put it, of "growing up absurd" plague everyone in a community—problems that are even more serious today than they were in the alienated 1960s decade. These transclass issues can bring people together with workers of all kinds in a common effort to seek their self-empowerment, an issue that cannot be resolved into the conflict of wage labor against capital alone.

Nor are workers mere "agents" of history, as vulgar Marxists (and implicitly, syndicalists) would have us believe. Workers live in cities, towns, and villages—not only as class beings but as civic beings. They are fathers and mothers, brothers and sisters, friends and comrades, and no less than their ecological counterparts among the petty bourgeoisie, they are concerned with environmental issues. As parents and young people, they are concerned with the problems of acquiring an education, entering a profession, and the like. They are deeply disturbed by the decay of urban infrastructures, the diminution of inexpensive housing, and issues of urban safety and aesthetics. Their horizon extends far beyond the realm of the factory or even the office to the residential urban world in which they and their families live. After I had spent years working in factories, I was not surprised to find that I could reach workers, middle-class people, and even relatively affluent individuals more easily by discussing issues relating to their lived environments—their neighborhoods and cities—rather than to their workplaces.

Today, in particular, the globalization of capital raises the question of how localities can keep productive resources within their own confines without impairing the opportunities of peoples in the so-called "Third World" or South to freely develop technologically according to their own needs. This conundrum cannot be resolved by legislation and economic reforms. Capitalism is a compulsively expansive system. A modern market economy dictates that an enterprise must grow or die, and nothing will prevent capitalism from industrializing—more accurately, expanding—endlessly over the entire face of the planet whenever it is prepared to do so. Only the complete reconstruction of society and the economy can end the dilemmas that globalization raises—the exploitation of workers and the enhancement of corporate power to the point of threatening the stability, indeed the very safety, of the planet.

Here again, I would contend that only a grassroots economic policy, based on a libertarian municipalist agenda and movement, can offer a major alternative—and it is precisely an alternative that many people seek today—capable of arresting the impact of globalization. For the problem of globalization, there is no global solution. Global capital, precisely because of its very hugeness, can only be eaten away at its roots, specifically by means of a libertarian municipalist resistance at the base of society. It must be eroded by the myriad millions who, mobilized by a grassroots movement, challenge global capital's sovereignty over their lives and try to develop local and regional economic alternatives to its industrial operations. Developing this resistance would involve subsidizing municipally controlled industries and retail outlets, and taking recourse in regional resources that capital does not find it profitable to use. A municipalized economy, slow as it may be in the making, will be a moral economy, one that—concerned primarily with the quality of its products and their production at the lowest possible cost—can hope to ultimately subvert a corporate economy, whose success is measured entirely by its profits rather than by the quality of its commodities.

Let me stress that when I speak of a moral economy, I am not advocating a communitarian or cooperative economy in which small profiteers, however well-meaning their intentions may be, simply become little "self-managed" capitalists in their own right. In my own community, I have seen a self-styled "moral" enterprise, Ben and Jerry's Ice Cream, grow in typical capitalist fashion from a small, presumably "caring," and intimate enterprise into a global corporation, intent on making profit and fostering the myth that "capitalism can be good." Cooperatives that profess to be moral in their intentions have yet to make any headway in replacing big capitalist concerns or even in surviving without themselves becoming capitalistic in their methods and profit-oriented in their goals.

The Proudhonist myth that small associations of producers—as opposed to a genuinely socialistic or libertarian communistic endeavor—can slowly eat away at capitalism should finally be dispelled. Sadly, these generally failed illusions are still promoted by liberals, anarchists, and academics alike. Either municipalized enterprises controlled by citizens' assemblies will try to take over the economy, or capitalism will prevail in this sphere of life with a forcefulness that no mere rhetoric can diminish.

Capitalist society has effects not only on economic and social relations but on ideas and intellectual traditions as well, indeed, on all of history, fragmenting them until knowledge, discourse, and even reality become blurred, divested of any distinctions, specificity, and articulation. The culture that promotes this celebration of diffuseness and fragmentation—a culture that is epidemic in American colleges and universities—goes under the name of poststructuralism or, more commonly, postmodernism. Given its corrosive precepts, the postmodernist worldview is able to level or homogenize everything that is unique or distinctive, dissolving it into a lowest common denominator of ideas.

Consider, for example, the obscurantist term "earth citizenship," which dissolves the very complex notion of "citizenship," with its presuppositions of *paideia*, that is, the lifelong education of the citizen for the practice of civic self-management, into a diffuse category, by extending (and cheapening) the notion of citizenship to include animals, plants, rocks, mountains, the planet, indeed the very cosmos itself. With a purely metaphorical label for all relationships as an "earth community," the historical and contemporary uniqueness of the city disappears. It presumably preempts every other community because of its wider scope and breadth. Such metaphors ultimately flatten everything, in effect, into a universal "Oneness" that, in the name of "ecological wisdom," denies definition to vital concepts and realities by the very ubiquity of the "One."

If the word "citizen" applies to every existing thing, and if the word "community" embraces all relationships in this seemingly "green" world, then nothing, in fact, is a citizen or a community.

Just as the logical category "Being" is rendered as mere existence, Being can only be regarded as interchangeable with "Nothing." So, too, "citizen" and "community" become a universal passport to vacuity, not to uniquely civic conditions that have been forming and differentiating dialectically for thousands of years through the ancient, medieval, and modern worlds. To reduce them to an abstract "community" is to ultimately negate their wealth of evolutionary forms and particularly their differentiation as sophisticated aspects of human freedom.

Libertarian municipalism must be conceived as a process, a patient practice that will have only limited success at the present time, and even then only in select areas that can at best provide examples of the possibilities it could hold if and when adopted on a large scale. We will not create a libertarian municipalist society overnight, and in this era of counterrevolution, we must be prepared to endure more failures than successes. Patience and commitment are traits that revolutionaries of the past cultivated assiduously; alas, today, in our fast consumerist society, the demand for immediate gratification, for fast food and fast living, inculcates a demand for fast politics. What should count for us is whether libertarian municipalism is a means for achieving the rational culmination of human development, not whether it is suitable as a quick fix for present social problems.

We must learn to be flexible without allowing our basic principles to be replaced by a postmodernist quagmire of ad hoc, ever-changeable opinions. For example, if we have no choice but to use electronic means, such as to establish popular participation in relatively large citizens' assemblies, then so be it. But we should, I would argue, do so only when it is unavoidable and for only as long as it is necessary. By the same token, if certain measures involve a degree of centralization, then we should adopt them—without sacrificing, let me insist, the right to immediate recall. But here, too, we should endure such organizational measures for only as long as they are necessary and no longer. Our basic principles in such cases must always be our guide: we remain committed to a direct face-to-face democracy and a well-coordinated, confederal, but decentralized society.

Nor should we fetishize consensus over democracy in our decision-making processes. Consensus, as I have argued, is practicable with very small groups in which people know each other intimately. But in larger groups, it becomes tyrannical because it allows a small minority to decide the practice of large or even sizable majority; and it fosters homogeneity and stagnation in ideas and policies. Minorities and their factions are the indispensable yeast for maturing new ideas—and nearly all new ideas start out as the views of minorities. In a libertarian group, the "rule" of the majority over a minority is a myth; no one expects a minority to give up its unpopular beliefs or to yield its right to argue its views—but the minority must have patience and allow a majority decision to be put into practice. This experience and the discussion it generates should be the most decisive element in impelling a group or assembly to reconsider its decision and adopt the minority's viewpoint, spurring on the further innovation of practices and ideas as other minorities emerge. Consensus decision-making can easily produce intellectual and practical stagnation if it essentially compels a majority to forgo a specific policy in order to please a minority.

I will not enter into my distinction between policy decisions and their enactment in practice by those qualified to administer them. I will only note that if the U.S. Congress—a gathering, for the most part, of lawyers—can make basic policy decisions on the reconstruction of the American infrastructure, on war and peace, on education and foreign policy, etc., without having full knowledge of all aspects of these fields, leaving the administration of their decisions to others, then I fail to understand why a citizens' assembly cannot make policy decisions on usually more modest issues and leave their administration, under close supervision, to experts in the fields involved.

Among the other issues that we must at some point consider are the place of law or *nomos* in a libertarian municipalist society, as well as constitutions that lay down important principles of right or justice and freedom. Are we to vest the perpetuation of our guiding principles simply in blind custom, or in the good nature of our fellow humans—which allows for a great deal of arbitrariness? For centuries, oppressed peoples demanded written founding constitutional provisions to protect them from the arbitrary oppression of the nobility. With the emergence of a libertarian communist society, this problem does not disappear. For us, I believe, the question can never be whether law and constitutions are inherently anti-anarchistic, but whether they are rational, mutable, secular, and restrictive only in the sense that they prohibit the abuse of power. We must, I believe, free ourselves of the fetishes born of remote polemics with authoritarians, fetishes that have pushed many anarchist communists into unreflective one-sided positions that are more like dogmas than reasoned theoretical ideas.

Admittedly, the present time is not one that is favorable for the spread of anticapitalist, social anarchist ideas and movements. Unless we are to let the capitalist cancer spread over the entire planet, however, even absorbing the natural world into the world economy, anarchist communists must develop a theory and practice that provides them with an entry into the public sphere—a theory and practice, I should emphasize, that is consistent with the goal of a rational, libertarian communist society.

Finally, we must assert the historic right of speculative reason, resting on the real potentialities of human beings as we know them from the past as well as the present, to project itself beyond the immediate environment in which we live, indeed, to claim that the present irrational society is not the actual—or "real"—that is worthy of the human condition. Despite its prevalence—and, to many people, its permanence—it is untrue to the project of fulfilling humanity's potentiality for freedom and self-consciousness, and hence it is unreal in the sense that it is a betrayal of the claims of humanity's greatest qualities, the capacity for reason and innovation.

By the same token, that broad school of ideas that we call

"anarchism" is faced with a parting of the ways between social anarchists, who wish to focus their efforts on the revolutionary elimination of hierarchical and class society, and individualist anarchists, who see social change only in terms of their personal self-expression and the replacement of serious ideas with mystical fantasies.

I personally do not believe that anarchism can become a public movement unless it formulates a politics that opens it to social intervention, that brings it into the public sphere as an organized movement that can grow, think rationally, mobilize people, and actively seek to change the world. The social democrats have offered us parliamentary reforms as a practice, and the results they have produced have been debilitating—most notably, a radical decline in public life and a disastrous growth in consumerist self-indulgence and privatism. Although the Stalinists as architects of the totalitarian state have mostly passed from the public scene, a few persist as parasites on whatever radical movement may emerge among oppressed peoples. And fascism, in its various mutations, has attempted to fill the void created by disempowerment and a lack of human scale in politics as well as community, with tragic results.

As anarchist communists, we must ask ourselves what mode of entry into the public sphere is consistent with our vision of empowerment. If our ideal is the Commune of communes, then I submit that the only means of entry and social fulfillment is a Communalist politics with a libertarian municipalist praxis; that is, a movement and program that finally emerges on the local political scene as the uncompromising advocate of popular neighborhood and town assemblies and the development of a municipalized economy. I know of no other alternative to capitulation to the existing society.

Libertarian municipalism is not a new version of reformism in the vein of Paul Brousse's "possibilism" of the 1890s. Rather, it is an explicit attempt to update the traditional social anarchist ideal of the Federation of communes or "Commune of communes," namely, the confederal linking of libertarian communist municipalities, in the form of directly democratic popular assemblies as well as the collective control or "ownership" of socially important property. Libertarian municipalism in no way compromises with parliamentarism, reformist attempts to "improve" capitalism or the perpetuation of private property. Limited exclusively to the municipality as the locus for political activity, as distinguished from provincial and state governments, not to speak of national and supranational governments, libertarian municipalism is revolutionary to the core, in the very important sense that it seeks to exacerbate the latent and often very real tension between the municipality and the state, and to enlarge the democratic institutions of the commune that still remain, at the expense of statist institutions. It counterposes the confederation to the nation-state, and libertarian communism to existing systems of private and nationalized property.

Where most anarchist communists in the past have regarded the Federation of communes as an ideal to be achieved after an insurrection, libertarian municipalists, I contend, regard the federation or confederation of communes as a political practice that can be developed, at least partly, prior to an outright revolutionary confrontation with the state—a confrontation which, in my view, cannot be avoided and, if anything, should be encouraged by increasing the tension between the state and federations of municipalities. In fact, libertarian municipalism is a communalist practice for creating a revolutionary culture and for bringing revolutionary change into complete conformity with the goals of anarchist communism.

In the last case, it unifies practice and ideal into a single and coherent means-and-ends approach for initiating a libertarian communist society, without any disjunction between the strategy for achieving such a society and the society itself. Nor does libertarian municipalism cultivate the illusion that the state and bourgeoisie will allow such a continuum to find fulfillment without open struggle, as some advocates of so-called "confederal municipalism" and "localist politics" have argued.

I have no doubt that libertarian municipalism, if it meets with a measure of success, will face many obstacles and the possibility of being co-opted or of degenerating into a form of "sewer anarchism," that it will face not only a civic realm of ideological discord but internal discord within its own organizational framework, that it opens a broad field of political conflict, with all its risks and uncertainties. At a time when social life has been trivialized beyond description, when accommodation to capitalist values and lifeways has reached unprecedented levels, when anarchism and socialism are seen as the "lost causes" of the nineteenth and early twentieth centuries, one can only hope that such discord becomes a genuine public reality. At no time has mediocrity been more triumphant than it is today, and at no time has indifference to social and political issues been as widespread as it is today.

I do not believe that social change can be achieved without taking risks, allowing for uncertainties, and recognizing the possibility of failure. If we are to have any effect on the fossilization of public life—to the extent that the present period is marked in any sense by a genuine public life—history too must move with us. On this score, I am much too old to make worthwhile predictions about how the course of events will unfold, except to say that the present, whether for good or ill, will hardly be recognizable to the generation that will come of age fifty years from now, so rapidly are things likely to change in the coming century.

But where change exists, so too do possibilities. The times cannot remain as they are, any more than the world can be frozen into immobility. What we can hope to do is to preserve the thread of rationality that distinguishes true civilization from barbarism—and barbarism would indeed be the outcome of a world that is permitted to tumble into a future without rational activity or guidance.

August 1998

4

The Meaning of Confederalism

Few arguments have been used more effectively to challenge the case for face-to-face participatory democracy than the claim that we live in a "complex society." Modern population centers, we are told, are too large and too concentrated to allow for direct decision-making at a grassroots level. And our economy is too "global," presumably, to unravel the intricacies of production and commerce. In our present transnational, often highly centralized social system, it is better to enhance representation in the state, to increase the efficiency of bureaucratic institutions, we are advised, than to advance utopian "localist" schemes of popular control over political and economic life.

After all, such arguments often run, centralists are all really "localists" in the sense that they believe in "more power to the people"—or at least, to their representatives. And surely a good representative is always eager to know the wishes of his or her "constituents" (to use another of those arrogant substitutes for "citizens").

But face-to-face democracy? Forget the dream that in our "complex" modern world we can have any democratic alternative to the nation-state! Many pragmatic people, including socialists, often dismiss arguments for that kind of "localism" as otherworldly—with good-natured condescension at best and outright derision at worst.

Indeed, some years back, in 1972, I was challenged in the periodical *Root and Branch* by Jeremy Brecher, a democratic socialist, to explain how the decentralist views I expressed in my 1969 essay "Post-Scarcity Anarchism" would prevent, say, Troy, New York, from dumping its untreated wastes into the Hudson River, from which downstream cities like Perth Amboy draw their drinking water.

On the surface of things, arguments like Brecher's for centralized government seem rather compelling. A structure that is "democratic," to be sure, but still largely top-down, is assumed as necessary to prevent one locality from afflicting another ecologically. But conventional economic and political arguments against decentralization, ranging from the fate of Perth Amboy's drinking water to our alleged "addiction" to petroleum, rest on a number of very problematical assumptions. Most disturbingly, they rest on an unconscious acceptance of the economic status quo.

DECENTRALISM AND SELF-SUSTAINABILITY

The assumption that what currently exists must necessarily exist is the acid that corrodes all visionary thinking (as witness the recent tendency of radicals to espouse "market socialism" rather than deal with the failings of the market economy as well as state socialism). Doubtless, we will have to import coffee for those people who need a morning fix at the breakfast table or exotic metals for people who want their wares to be more lasting than the junk produced by a consciously engineered throwaway economy. But aside from the utter irrationality of crowding tens of millions of people into congested, indeed, suffocating urban belts, must the present-day extravagant international division of labor necessarily exist in order to satisfy human needs? Or has it been created to provide extravagant profits for multinational corporations? Are we to ignore the ecological consequences of plundering the Third World of its resources, insanely interlocking modern economic life with petroleum-rich areas whose ultimate products include air pollutants and petroleum-derived carcinogens? To ignore the fact that our "global economy" is the result of burgeoning industrial bureaucracies and a competitive grow-or-die market economy is profoundly myopic.

It is hardly necessary to explore the sound ecological reasons for achieving a certain measure of self-sustainability. Most environmentally oriented people are aware that a massive national and international division of labor is extremely wasteful in the literal sense of that term. Not only does an excessive division of labor make for overorganization in the form of huge bureaucracies and tremendous expenditures of resources in transporting materials over great distances, it reduces the possibilities of effectively recycling wastes, avoiding pollution that may have its source in highly concentrated industrial and population centers, and making sound use of local or regional raw materials.

On the other hand, we cannot ignore the fact that relatively self-sustaining communities in which crafts, agriculture, and industries serve definable networks of confederally organized communities enrich the opportunities and stimuli to which individuals are exposed and make for more rounded personalities with a rich sense of selfhood and competence. The Greek ideal of the rounded citizen in a rounded environment—one that reappeared in Charles Fourier's utopian works—was long cherished by the anarchists and socialists of the last century.

The opportunity of the individual to devote his or her productive activity to many different tasks over an attenuated work week (or in Fourier's ideal society, over a given day) was seen as a vital factor in overcoming the division between manual and intellectual activity, in transcending status differences that this major division of work created, and in enhancing the wealth of experiences that came with a free movement from industry through crafts to food cultivation. Hence, self-sustainability made for a richer self, one strengthened by variegated experiences, competencies, and assurances. Alas, this vision was lost by leftists and many environmentalists in the second half of the twentieth century, with their shift toward a pragmatic liberalism and the radical movement's tragic ignorance of its own visionary past.

We should not, I believe, lose sight of what it means to live an ecological way of life, not merely follow sound ecological practices. The multitude of handbooks that teach us how to conserve, invest, eat, and buy in an "ecologically responsible" manner are a travesty of the more basic need to reflect on what it means to think—yes, to reason—and to live ecologically in the full meaning of the term. Thus, I would hold that to garden organically is more than a good form of husbandry and a good source of nutrients; it is above all a way to place oneself directly in the food web by personally cultivating the very substances one consumes to live and by returning to one's environment what one elicits from it.

Food thus becomes more than a form of material nutrient. The soil one tills, the living things one cultivates and consumes, the compost one prepares all unite in an ecological continuum to feed the spirit as well as the body, sharpening one's sensitivity to the nonhuman and human world around us. I am often amused by zealous "spiritualists," many of whom are either passive viewers of seemingly "natural" landscapes or devotees of rituals, magic, and pagan deities (or all of these) who fail to realize that one of the most eminently human activities, namely, food cultivation, can do more to foster an ecological sensibility (and spirituality, if you please) than all the incantations and mantras devised in the name of ecological spiritualism.

Such monumental changes as the dissolution of the nation-state and its substitution by a participatory democracy, then, do not occur in a psychological vacuum where the political structure alone is changed. I argued against Jeremy Brecher that in a society that was radically veering toward decentralistic, participatory democracy, guided by communitarian and ecological principles, it is only reasonable to suppose that people would not choose such an irresponsible social dispensation as would allow the waters of the Hudson to be so polluted. Decentralism, a face-to-face participatory democracy, and a localist emphasis on community values should be viewed as all of one piece—they most assuredly have been so in the vision I have been advocating for more than thirty years.

This "one piece" involves not only a new politics but a new political culture that embraces new ways of thinking and feeling, and new human interrelationships, including the ways we experience the natural world. Words like "politics" and "citizenship" would be redefined by the rich meanings they acquired in the past, and enlarged for the present.

It is not very difficult to show, item by item, how the international division of labor can be greatly attenuated by using local and regional resources, implementing ecotechnologies, rescaling human consumption along rational (indeed, healthful) lines, and emphasizing quality production that provides lasting (instead of throwaway) means of life. It is unfortunate that the very considerable inventory of these possibilities, which I partly assembled and evaluated in my 1965 essay "Toward a Liberatory Technology," suffers from the burden of having been written too long ago to be accessible to the present generation of ecologically oriented people. Indeed, in that essay, I also argued for regional integration and the need to interlink resources among ecocommunities; for decentralized communities are inevitably interdependent upon one another.

PROBLEMS OF DECENTRALISM

If many pragmatic people are blind to the importance of decentralism, many in the ecology movement tend to ignore very real problems with "localism"—problems that are no less troubling than the problems raised by a globalism that fosters a total interlocking of economic and political life on a worldwide basis. Without such holistic cultural and political changes, notions of decentralism that emphasize localist isolation and a degree of self-sufficiency may lead to cultural parochialism and chauvinism. Parochialism can lead to problems that are as serious as a "global" mentality that overlooks the uniqueness of cultures, the peculiarities of ecosystems and ecoregions, and the need for a humanly scaled community life that makes a participatory democracy possible. This is no minor issue today, in an ecology movement that tends to swing toward very well-meaning but rather naïve extremes. I cannot repeat too emphatically that we must find a way of sharing the world with other humans and with nonhuman forms of life, a view that is often difficult to attain in overly "self-sufficient" communities.

Much as I respect the intentions of those who advocate local self-reliance and self-sustainability, these concepts can be highly misleading. I can certainly agree with the assertion, for example, that if a community can produce the things it needs, it should probably do so. But self-sustaining communities cannot produce all the things they need—unless it involves a return to a back-breaking way of village life that historically often prematurely aged its men and women with hard work and allowed them very little time for political life beyond the immediate confines of the community itself.

I regret to say that there are people in the ecology movement who do, in fact, advocate a return to a highly labor-intensive economy, not to speak of Stone Age deities. Clearly, we must give the ideals of localism, decentralism, and self-sustainability greater and fuller meaning.

Today, we can produce the basic means of life—and a good deal more—in an ecological society that is focused on the production of high-quality useful goods. Yet still others in the ecology movement too often end up advocating a kind of "cooperative" capitalism, in which one community functions like a single entrepreneur, with a sense of proprietorship toward its resources. Such a system of cooperatives once again marks the beginnings of a market system of distribution as cooperatives become entangled in the web of "bourgeois rights," that is, in contracts and bookkeeping that focus on the exact amounts a community will receive in "exchange" for what it delivers to others. This deterioration occurred among some of the worker-controlled enterprises that functioned like capitalistic enterprises in Barcelona after the workers expropriated them in July 1936—a practice that the anarchosyndicalist CNT fought early in the Spanish Revolution.

It is a troubling fact that neither decentralization nor self-sufficiency in itself is necessarily democratic. Plato's ideal city in the Republic was, indeed, designed to be self-sufficient, but its self-sufficiency was meant to maintain a warrior as well as a philosophical elite. Indeed, its capacity to preserve its self-sufficiency depended upon its ability, like Sparta, to resist the seemingly "corruptive" influence of outside cultures. Similarly, decentralization in itself provides no assurance that we will have an ecological society. A decentralized society can easily coexist with extremely rigid hierarchies. A striking example is European and Oriental feudalism, a social order in which princely, ducal, and baronial hierarchies were based on highly decentralized communities. With all due respect to Fritz Schumacher, small is not necessarily beautiful.

Nor does it follow that humanly scaled communities and "appropriate technologies" in themselves constitute guarantees against domineering societies. In fact, for centuries, humanity lived in villages and small towns, often with tightly organized social ties and even communistic forms of property. But these provided the material basis for highly despotic imperial states. Considered on economic and property terms, they might earn a high place in the "no-growth" outlook of economists like Herman Daly, but they were the hard bricks that were used to build the most awesome despotisms in India and China. What these self-sufficient, decentralized communities feared almost as much as the armies that ravaged them were the imperial tax-gatherers that plundered them.

If we extol such communities because of the extent to which they were decentralized, self-sufficient, or small, or employed "appropriate technologies," we would be obliged to ignore the extent to which they were also culturally stagnant and easily dominated by exogenous elites. Their seemingly organic but tradition-bound division of labor may very well have formed the bases for highly oppressive and degrading caste systems in different parts of the world—caste systems that plague the social life of India to this very day.

At the risk of seeming contrary, I feel obliged to emphasize that decentralization, localism, self-sufficiency, and even confederation, each taken singly, do not constitute a guarantee that we will achieve a rational ecological society. In fact, all of them have at one time or another supported parochial communities, oligarchies, and even despotic regimes. To be sure, without the institutional structures that cluster around our use of these terms and without taking them in combination with each other, we cannot hope to achieve a free ecologically oriented society.

CONFEDERALISM AND INTERDEPENDENCE

Decentralism and self-sustainability must involve a much broader principle of social organization than mere localism. Together with decentralization, approximations to self-sufficiency, humanly scaled communities, ecotechnologies, and the like, there is a compelling need for democratic and truly communitarian forms of interdependence—in short, for libertarian forms of confederalism.

I have detailed at length in many articles and books (particularly *From Urbanization to Cities*) the history of confederal structures from ancient and medieval to modern confederations such as the *Comuñeros* in the early sixteenth century through the Parisian sectional movement of 1793 and more recent attempts at confederation, particularly by the Anarchists in the Spanish Revolution of the 1930s. Today, what often leads to serious misunderstandings among decentralists is their failure in all too many cases to see the need for confederation, which at least tends to counteract the tendency of decentralized communities to drift toward exclusivity and parochialism. If we lack a clear understanding of what confederalism means—indeed, the fact that it forms a key principle and gives fuller meaning to decentralism—a libertarian municipalist agenda can easily become vacuous at best or be used for highly parochial ends at worst.

What, then, is confederalism? It is above all a network of administrative councils whose members or delegates are elected from popular face-to-face democratic assemblies, in the various villages, towns, and even neighborhoods of large cities. The members of these confederal councils are strictly mandated, recallable, and responsible to the assemblies that choose them for the purpose of coordinating and administering the policies formulated by the assemblies themselves. Their function is thus a purely administrative and practical one, not a policymaking one like the function of representatives in republican systems of government.

A confederalist view involves a clear distinction between policymaking and the coordination and execution of adopted policies. Policymaking is exclusively the right of popular community assemblies based on the practices of participatory democracy. Administration and coordination are the responsibility of confederal councils, which become the means for interlinking villages, towns, neighborhoods, and cities into confederal networks. Power thus flows from the bottom up instead of from the top down, and in confederations, the flow of power from the bottom up diminishes with the scope of the federal council ranging territorially from localities to regions and from regions to ever-broader territorial areas.

A crucial element in giving reality to confederalism is the interdependence of communities for an authentic mutualism based on shared resources, production, and policymaking. If one community is not obliged to count on another or others generally to satisfy important material needs and realize common political goals in such a way that it is interlinked to a greater whole, exclusivity and parochialism are genuine possibilities. Only insofar as we recognize that confederation must be conceived as an extension of a form of participatory administration—by means of confederal networks—can decentralization and localism prevent the communities that compose larger bodies of association from withdrawing into themselves at the expense of wider areas of human consociation.

Confederalism is thus a way of perpetuating the interdependence that should exist among communities and regions; indeed, it is a way of democratizing that interdependence without surrendering the principle of local control. While a reasonable measure of self-sufficiency is desirable for every locality and region, confeder-alism is a means for avoiding local parochialism on the one hand and an extravagant national and global division of labor on the other. In short, it is a way in which a community can retain its identity and roundedness while participating in a sharing way with the larger whole that makes up a balanced ecological society.

Confederalism as a principle of social organization reaches its fullest development when the economy itself is confederalized by placing local farms, factories, and other needed enterprises in local municipal hands; that is, when a community, however large or small, begins to manage its own economic resources in an inter-linked network with other communities. To force a choice between either self-sufficiency on the one hand or a market system of exchange on the other is a simplistic and unnecessary dichotomy. I would like to think that a confederal ecological society would be a sharing one—one based on the pleasure that is felt in distributing among communities according to their needs, not one in which "cooperative" capitalistic communities mire themselves in the quid pro quo of exchange relationships.

Impossible? Unless we are to believe that nationalized property (which reinforces the political power of the centralized state with economic power) or a private market economy (whose law of "grow or die" threatens to undermine the ecological stability of the entire planet) is more workable, I fail to see what viable alternative we have to the confederated municipalization of the economy. At any rate, for once, it will no longer be privileged state bureaucrats or grasping bourgeois entrepreneurs—or even "collective" capitalists in so-called "workers-controlled enterprises"—all with their special interests to promote, who are faced with a community's problems, but citizens, irrespective of their occupations or workplaces. For once, it will be necessary to transcend the traditional special inter-ests of work, workplace, status, and property relations, and create a general interest based on shared community problems.

Confederation is thus the ensemble of decentralization, localism, self-sufficiency, interdependence—and more. This more is the indispensable moral education and character building—what the Greeks called *paideia*—that makes for rational active citizenship in a participatory democracy, unlike the passive constituents and consumers that we have today. In the end, there is no substitute for a conscious reconstruction of our relationship to each other and the natural world.

To argue that the remaking of society and our relationship with the natural world can be achieved merely by decentralization or localism or self-sustainability leaves us with an incomplete collection of solutions. Whatever we omit among these presuppositions for a society based on confederated municipalities would leave a yawning hole in the entire social fabric we hope to create. That hole would grow and eventually destroy the fabric itself, just as a market economy, conjoined with "socialism," "anarchism," or whatever concept one has of the good society, would eventually dominate the society as a whole. Nor can we omit the distinction between policymaking and administration, for once policymaking slips from the hands of the people, it is devoured by its delegates, who quickly become bureaucrats.

Confederalism, in effect, must be conceived as a whole: a consciously formed body of interdependencies that unites participatory democracy in municipalities with a scrupulously supervised system of coordination. It involves the dialectical development of independence and dependence into a more richly articulated form of interdependence, just as the individual in a free society grows from dependence in childhood to independence in youth, only to sublate the two into a conscious form of interdependence between individuals and between the individual and society.

Confederalism is thus a fluid and ever-developing kind of social metabolism in which the identity of an ecological society is preserved through its differences and by virtue of its potential for ever-greater differentiation. Confederalism, in fact, does not mark a closure of social history (as the "end of history" ideologists of recent years would have us believe about liberal capitalism) but rather the point of departure for a new ecosocial history marked by a participatory evolution within society and between society and the natural world.

CONFEDERATION AS DUAL POWER

Above all, I have tried to show in my previous writings how confederation on a municipal basis has existed in sharp tension with the centralized state generally and the nation-state of recent times. Confederalism, I have tried to emphasize, is not simply a unique societal, particularly civic, or municipal, form of administration. It is a vibrant tradition in the affairs of humanity, one that has a centuries-long history behind it. For generations, confederations tried to countervail a nearly equally long historical tendency toward centralization and the creation of the nation-state.

If the two—confederalism and statism—are not seen as being in tension with each other, a tension in which the nation-state has used a variety of intermediaries like provincial governments in Canada and state governments in the United States to create the illusion of "local control," then the concept of confederation loses all meaning. Provincial autonomy in Canada and states' rights in the United States are no more confederal than "soviets" or councils were the medium for popular control that existed in tension with Stalin's totalitarian state. The Russian soviets were taken over by the Bolsheviks, who supplanted them with their party within a year or two of the October Revolution. To weaken the role of confederal municipalities as a countervailing power to the nation-state by opportunistically running "confederalist" candidates for state government—or, more nightmarishly, for governorship in seemingly democratic states (as some U.S. Greens have proposed)—is to blur the importance of the need for tension between confederations and nation-states; indeed, they obscure the fact that the two cannot coexist over the long term.

In describing confederalism—as a structure for decentralization, participatory democracy, and localism—and as a potentiality for an ever-greater differentiation along new lines of development,

I would like to emphasize that this same concept of wholeness that applies to the interdependencies between municipalities also applies to the municipality itself. The municipality, as I have pointed out in earlier writings, is the most immediate political arena of the individual—the world that is literally a doorstep beyond the privacy of the family and the intimacy of personal friendships. In that primary political arena, where politics should be conceived in the Hellenic sense of literally managing the polis or community, the individual can be transformed from a mere person into an active citizen—from a private being into a public being. Given this crucial arena that renders citizens able to participate directly in the future of society, we are dealing with a level of human interaction that is more basic (apart from the family itself) than any level that is expressed in representative forms of governance where collective power is literally transmuted into power embodied by one or a few individuals. The municipality is thus the most authentic arena of public life, however much it may have been distorted over the course of history.

By contrast, delegated or authoritarian levels of "politics" presuppose the abdication of municipal and citizen power to one degree or another. The municipality must always be understood as this truly authentic public world. To compare even executive positions, like a mayor with a governor, in representative realms of power is to grossly misunderstand the basic political nature of civic life itself, all its malformations notwithstanding. Thus, for Greens to contend in a purely formal and analytical manner—as modern logic instructs that terms like "executive" make the two positions interchangeable—is to totally remove the notion of executive power from its context, to reify it, to make it into a lifeless category because of the external trappings we attach to the word. If the city is to be seen as a whole, and its potentialities for creating a participatory democracy are to be fully recognized, then provincial and state governments in Canada and the United States must be seen as small republics organized entirely around representation at best and oligarchical rule at worst. They provide the channels of expression for the nation-state—and constitute obstacles to the development of a genuine public realm.

To run a Green for a mayor on a libertarian municipalist program, in short, is qualitatively different from running a provincial or state governor on a presumably libertarian muncipalist program. It amounts to decontextualizing the institutions that exist in a municipality, in a province or state, and in the nation-state itself, thereby placing all three of these executive positions under a purely formal rubric. One might with equal imprecision say that because human beings and dinosaurs both have spinal cords, that they belong to the same species or even to the same genus. In each such case, an institution—be it a mayoral, councillor, or selectperson—must be seen in a municipal context as a whole, just as a president, prime minister, congressperson, or member of parliament, in turn, must be seen in the state context as a whole. From this standpoint, for Greens to run mayors is fundamentally different from running for provincial and state offices. One can go into endless detailed reasons why the powers of a mayor are far more controlled and under closer public purview than those of state and provincial office-holders.

To ignore this fact is to abandon any sense of contextuality and the environment in which issues like policy, administration, participation, and representation must be placed. Simply, a city hall in a town or city is not a capital in a province, state, or nation-state.

Unquestionably, there are now cities that are so large that they verge on being quasi-republics in their own right. One thinks, for example, of such megalopolitan areas as New York City and Los Angeles. In such cases, the minimal program of a Green movement can demand that confederations be established within the urban area—namely, among neighborhoods or definable districts—not only among the urban areas themselves. In a very real sense, these highly populated, sprawling, and oversized entities must ultimately be broken down institutionally into municipalities that are scaled to human dimensions and that lend themselves to participatory democracy. These entities are not yet fully formed state powers, either institutionally or in reality, such as we find even in sparsely populated American states. The mayor is not yet a governor, with the enormous coercive powers that a governor has, nor is the city council a parliament or statehouse that can literally legislate the death penalty into existence, such as is occurring in the United States today.

In cities that are transforming themselves into quasi-states, there is still a good deal of leeway in which politics can be conducted along libertarian lines. Already, the executive branches of these urban entities constitute a highly precarious ground, burdened by enormous bureaucracies, police powers, tax powers, and juridical systems that raise serious problems for a libertarian municipal approach. We must always ask ourselves in all frankness what form the concrete situation takes. Where city councils and mayoral offices in large cities provide an arena for battling the concentration of power in an increasingly strong state or provincial executive, and even worse, in regional jurisdictions that may cut across many such cities (Los Angeles is a notable example), to run candidates for the city council may be the only recourse we have for arresting the development of increasingly authoritarian state institutions and helping to restore an institutionally decentralized democracy.

It will no doubt take a long time to physically decentralize an urban entity such as New York City into authentic municipalities and ultimately communes. Such an effort is part of the maximum program of a Green movement. But there is no reason why an urban entity of such a huge magnitude cannot be slowly decentralized institutionally. The distinction between physical decentralization and institutional decentralization must always be kept in mind. Time and again, excellent proposals have been advanced by radicals and even city planners to localize democracy in such huge urban entities and give greater power to the people, only to be cynically shot down by centralists who invoke physical impediments to such an endeavor.

To make institutional decentralization congruent with the physical breakup of such a large entity confuses the arguments of advocates for decentralization. There is a certain treachery on the part of centralists in making these two very distinct lines of development identical or entangling them with each other. Libertarian municipalists must always keep the distinction between institutional and physical decentralization clearly in mind and recognize that the former is entirely achievable even while the latter may take years to attain.

November 1990

5

Libertarian Municipalism:
A Politics of Direct Democracy

Perhaps the greatest single failing of movements for social reconstruction—I refer particularly to the Left, to radical ecology groups, and to organizations that profess to speak for the oppressed—is their lack of a politics that will carry people beyond the limits established by the status quo.

Politics today primarily means duels between top-down bureaucratic parties for electoral office that offer vacuous programs for "social justice" to attract a nondescript "electorate." Once in office, their programs usually turn into a bouquet of "compromises." In this respect, many Green parties in Europe have been only marginally different from conventional parliamentary parties. Nor have socialist parties, with all their various labels, exhibited any basic differences from their capitalist counterparts. To be sure, the indifference of the Euro-American public—its "apoliticism"—is understandably depressing. Given their low expectations, when people do vote, they normally turn to established parties if only because, as centers of power, they can produce results, of sorts, in practical matters. If one bothers to vote, most people reason, why waste a vote on a new marginal organization that has all the characteristics of the major ones and will, if it succeeds, eventually become corrupted? Witness the German Greens, whose internal and public life increasingly approximates that of traditional parties.

That this "political process" has lingered on with almost no basic alteration for decades now is due in great part to the inertia of the process itself. Time wears expectations thin, and hopes are often reduced to habits as one disappointment is followed by another. Talk of a "new politics," of upsetting tradition, which is as old as politics itself, is becoming unconvincing. For decades, at least, the changes that have occurred in radical politics are largely changes in rhetoric rather than structure. The German Greens are only the most recent of a succession of "nonparty parties" (to use their original way of describing their organization) that have turned from an attempt to practice grassroots politics—ironically, in the Bundestag, of all places!—into a typical parliamentary party. The Social Democratic Party in Germany, the Labor Party in Britain, the New Democratic Party in Canada, the Socialist Party in France, and others, despite their original emancipatory visions, barely qualify today as even liberal parties in which a Franklin D. Roosevelt or a Harry Truman would have found a comfortable home. Whatever social ideals these parties may have had generations ago has been eclipsed by the pragmatics of gaining, holding, and extending their power in their respective parliamentary and ministerial bodies.

It is precisely such parliamentary and ministerial objectives that we call "politics" today. To the modern political imagination, "politics" is a body of techniques for holding power in representative bodies—notably the legislative and executive arenas—not a moral calling based on rationality, community, and freedom.

Libertarian municipalism represents a serious, indeed a historically fundamental project to render politics ethical in character and grassroots in organization. It is structurally and morally different from other grassroots efforts, not merely rhetorically different. It seeks to reclaim the public sphere for the exercise of authentic citizenship while breaking away from the bleak cycle of parliamentarism and its mystification of the "party" mechanism as a means for public representation. In these respects, libertarian municipalism is not merely a "political strategy." It is an effort to work from latent or incipient democratic possibilities toward a radically new configuration of society itself—a communal society oriented toward meeting human needs, responding to ecological imperatives, and developing a new ethics based on sharing and cooperation. That it involves a consistently independent form of politics is a truism. More important, it involves a redefinition of politics, a return to the word's original Greek meaning as the management of the community, or polis, by means of direct face-to-face assemblies of the people in the formulation of public policy and based on an ethics of complementarity and solidarity.

In this respect, libertarian municipalism is not one of many pluralistic techniques that is intended to achieve a vague and undefined social goal. Democratic to its core and nonhierarchical in its structure, it is a kind of human destiny, not merely one of an assortment of political tools or strategies that can be adopted and discarded with the aim of achieving power. Libertarian municipalism, in effect, seeks to define the institutional contours of a new society even as it advances the practical message of a radically new politics for our day.

Here, means and ends meet in a rational unity. The word politics now expresses direct popular control of society by its citizens through achieving and sustaining a true democracy in municipal assemblies—this, as distinguished from republican systems of representation that preempt the right of the citizen to formulate community and regional policies. Such politics is radically distinct from statecraft and the state—a professional body composed of bureaucrats, police, military, legislators, and the like that exists as a coercive apparatus, clearly distinct from and above the people. The libertarian municipalist approach distinguishes statecraft—which we usually characterize as "politics" today—and politics as it once existed in precapitalist democratic communities.

Moreover, libertarian municipalism also involves a clear deline-ation of the social realm—as well as the political realm—in the strict meaning of the term social: notably, the arena in which we live our private lives and engage in production. As such, the social realm is to be distinguished from both the political and the statist realms. Enormous harm has been caused by the interchangeable use of these terms—social, political, and the state. Indeed, the tendency has been to identify them with one another in our thinking and in the reality of everyday life. But the state is a completely alien formation, a thorn in the side of human development, an exogenous entity that has incessantly encroached on the social and political realms. In fact, the state has often been an end in itself, as witness the rise of Asian empires, ancient imperial Rome, and the totalitarian state of modern times. More than this, it has steadily invaded the political domain, which, for all its past shortcomings, had empowered com-munities, social groupings, and individuals.

Such invasions have not gone unchallenged. Indeed, the conflict between the state on the one hand and the political and social realms on the other has been an ongoing subterranean civil war for centuries. It has often broken out into the open—in modern times in the conflict of the Castilian cities (*Comuñeros*) against the Spanish monarchy in the 1520s, in the struggle of the Parisian sections against the centralist Jacobin Convention of 1793, and in endless other clashes both before and after these encounters.

Today, with the increasing centralization and concentration of power in the nation-state, a "new politics"—one that is genuinely new—must be structured institutionally around the restoration of power by municipalities. This is not only necessary but possible even in such gigantic urban areas as New York City, Montreal, London, and Paris. Such urban agglomerations are not, strictly speaking, cities or municipalities in the traditional sense of those terms, despite being designated as such by sociologists. It is only if we think that they are cities that we become mystified by problems of size and logistics. Even before we confront the ecological imper-ative of physical decentralization (a necessity anticipated by

Friedrich Engels and Peter Kropotkin alike), we need feel no problems about decentralizing them institutionally. When François Mitterand tried to decentralize Paris with local city halls some years ago, his reasons were strictly tactical—he wanted to weaken the authority of the capital's right-wing mayor. Nonetheless, he failed not because restructuring the large metropolis was impossible but because the majority of affluent Parisians supported the mayor.

Clearly, institutional changes do not occur in a social vacuum. Nor do they guarantee that a decentralized municipality, even if it is structurally democratic, will necessarily be humane, rational, and ecological in dealing with public affairs. Libertarian municipalism is premised on the struggle to achieve a rational and ecological society, a struggle that depends on education and organization. From the beginning, it presupposes a genuinely democratic desire by people to arrest the growing powers of the nation-state and reclaim them for their community and region. Unless there is a movement—hopefully an effective Left Green movement—to foster these aims, decentralization can lead to local parochialism as easily as it can lead to ecological, humanist communities.

But when have basic social changes ever been without risk? The case that Marx's commitment to a centralized state and planned economy would inevitably yield bureaucratic totalitarianism could have been better made than the case that decentralized libertarian municipalities will inevitably be authoritarian and have exclusionary and parochial traits. Economic interdependence is a fact of life today, and capitalism itself has made parochial autarchies a chimera. While municipalities and regions can seek to attain a considerable measure of self-sufficiency, we have long since left the era when it was still possible for self-sufficient communities to indulge their prejudices.

Equally important is the need for confederation—the networking of communities with one another through recallable deputies mandated by municipal citizens' assemblies and whose sole functions are coordinative and administrative. Confederation has a long history of its own that dates back to antiquity, which surfaced as a major alternative to the nation-state. From the American Revolution, through the French Revolution and the Spanish Revolution, confederalism has challenged state centralism. Nor has it disappeared in our own time, when the breakup of existing twentieth-century empires raises the issue of enforced state centralism or the relatively autonomous nation. Libertarian municipalism adds a radically democratic dimension to the contemporary discussions of confederation (as, for example, in the former Yugoslavia and Czechoslovakia) by calling for confederations not of nation-states but of municipalities and of the neighborhoods of giant megalopolitan areas as well as towns and villages.

In the case of libertarian municipalism, parochialism can thus be checked not only by the compelling realities of economic interdependence but by the commitment of municipal minorities to defer to the majority wishes of participating communities. Do these interdependencies and majority decisions guarantee us that a majority decision will be a correct one? Certainly not; but our chances for a rational and ecological society are much better in this approach than in those that ride on centralized entities and bureaucratic apparatuses. I cannot help but marvel that no municipal network has emerged among the German Greens, who have hundreds of representatives in city councils around Germany but who carry on a local politics that is largely conventional and self-enclosed within particular towns and cities.

Many arguments against libertarian municipalism—even with its strong confederal emphasis—derive from a failure to understand its distinction between policymaking and administration. This distinction is fundamental to libertarian municipalism and must always be kept in mind. Policy is made by a community or neighborhood assembly of free citizens; administration is performed by confederal councils composed of mandated, recallable deputies of wards, towns, and villages. If particular communities or neighborhoods (or a minority grouping of them) choose to go their own way to a point where human rights are violated or where ecological

mayhem is permitted, the majority in a local or regional confederation has every right to prevent such malfeasances through its
confederal council. This is not a denial of democracy but the assertion of a shared agreement by all to recognize civil rights and
maintain the ecological integrity of a region. These rights and needs
are not asserted so much by a confederal council as by the majority
of the popular assemblies conceived as one large community that
expresses its wishes through confederal deputies. Thus, policymaking still remains local, but its administration is vested in the
confederal network as a whole. In effect, the confederation is a
Community of communities, based on distinct human rights and
ecological imperatives.

If libertarian municipalism is not to be totally warped of its form
and divested of its meaning, it is a desideratum that must be fought
for. It speaks to a time (hopefully, one that will yet come) when
disempowered people actively seek empowerment. Existing in
growing tension with the nation-state, it is a process as well as a
struggle to be fulfilled, not a bequest granted by the summits of the
state. It is a dual power that contests the legitimacy of existing state
power. Such a movement can be expected to begin slowly, perhaps
sporadically, in communities that initially may demand only the
moral authority to alter the structure of society before enough inter-
linked confederations exist to demand the outright institutional
power to replace the state. The growing tension created by the emergence of municipal confederations represents a confrontation
between the state and the political realms. This confrontation can
be resolved only after libertarian municipalism forms the new politics of a popular movement and ultimately captures the imagination
of millions.

Certain points, however, should be obvious. The people who
initially enter into the duel between confederalism and statism
will not be the same human beings as those who eventually achieve
libertarian municipalism. The movement that tries to educate
them and the struggles that give libertarian municipalist principles
reality will turn them into active citizens rather than passive

"constituents." No one who participates in a struggle for social restructuring emerges from that struggle with the prejudices, habits, and sensibilities with which he or she entered it. Hopefully, such prejudices, like parochialism, will increasingly be replaced by a generous sense of cooperation and a caring sense of interdependence.

It remains to emphasize that libertarian municipalism is not merely an evocation of traditional antistatist notions of politics. Just as it redefines politics to include face-to-face municipal democracies graduated to confederal levels, so it includes a municipalist and confederal approach to economics. Minimally, a libertarian municipalist economics calls for the municipalization of the economy, not its centralization into state-owned "nationalized" enterprises on the one hand or its reduction to "worker-controlled" forms of collectivistic capitalism on the other. Trade-union-directed "worker-controlled" enterprises, that is, syndicalism, has had its day. This should be evident to anyone who examines the bureaucracies that even revolutionary trade unions spawned during the Spanish Civil War of 1936. Today, corporate capitalism is increasingly eager to bring workers into complicity with their own exploitation by means of "workplace democracy." Nor was the revolution in Spain and in other countries spared the existence of competition among worker-controlled enterprises for raw materials, markets, and profits. Even more recently, many Israeli kibbutzim have been failures as examples of nonexploitative, need-oriented enterprises, despite the high ideals with which they were initially founded.

Libertarian municipalism proposes a radically different form of economy—one that is neither nationalized nor collectivized according to syndicalist precepts. It proposes that land and enterprises be placed increasingly in the custody of the community—more precisely, the custody of citizens in free assemblies and their deputies in confederal councils. How work should be planned, what technologies should be used, how goods should be distributed are questions that can only be resolved in practice. The maxim "from each according to his or her ability, to each according to his or her needs" would seem a bedrock guide for an economically rational society, provided that goods are of the highest durability and quality, that needs are guided by rational and ecological standards, and that the ancient notions of limit and balance replace the bourgeois marketplace imperative of "grow or die."

In such a municipal economy—confederal, interdependent, and rational by ecological, not simply technological, standards—we would expect that the special interests that divide people today into workers, professionals, managers, and the like would be melded into a general interest in which people see themselves as citizens guided strictly by the needs of their community and region rather than by personal proclivities and vocational concerns. Here, citizenship would come into its own, and rational as well as ecological interpretations of the public good would supplant class and hierarchical interests.

This is the moral basis of a moral economy for moral communities. But of overarching importance is the general social interest that potentially underpins all moral communities, an interest that must ultimately cut across class, gender, ethnic, and status lines if humanity is to continue to exist as a viable species. In our times, this common interest is posed by ecological catastrophe. Capitalism's grow-or-die imperative stands radically at odds with ecology's imperative of interdependence and limit. The two imperatives can no longer coexist with each other; nor can any society founded on the myth that they can be reconciled hope to survive. Either we will establish an ecological society or society will go under for everyone, irrespective of his or her status.

Will this ecological society be authoritarian, or possibly even totalitarian, a hierarchical dispensation that is implicit in the image of the planet as a "spaceship"? Or will it be democratic? If history is any guide, the development of a democratic ecological society, as distinguished from a command ecological society, must follow its own logic. One cannot resolve this historical dilemma without getting to its roots. Without a searching analysis of our ecological problems and their social sources, the pernicious institutions that we have now will lead to increased centralization and further ecological catastrophe. In a democratic ecological society, those roots are literally the "grass-roots" that libertarian municipalism seeks to foster.

For those who rightly call for a new technology, new sources of energy, new means of transportation, and new ecological lifeways, can a new society be anything less than a Community of communities based on confederation rather than statism? We already live in a world in which the economy is overglobalized, overcentralized, and overbureaucratized. Much that can be done locally and region-ally is now being done—largely for profit, military needs, and imperial appetites—on a global scale with a seeming complexity that can actually be easily diminished.

If this seems too "utopian" for our time, then so must the present flood of literature that asks for radically sweeping shifts in energy policies, far-reaching reductions in air and water pollution, and the formulation of worldwide plans to arrest global warming and the destruction of the ozone layer. Is it too much to take such demands one step further and call for institutional and economic changes that are no less drastic and that, in fact, are deeply sedimented in the noblest democratic political traditions of both America and, indeed, the world?

Nor are we obliged to expect these changes to occur immediately. The Left long worked with minimum and maximum programs for change, in which immediate steps that can be taken now were linked by transitional advances and intermediate areas that would eventually yield ultimate goals. Minimal steps that can be taken now include initiating Left Green municipalist movements that propose popular neighborhood and town assemblies—even if they have only moral functions at first—and electing town and city councillors that advance the cause of these assemblies and other popular institutions. These minimal steps can progressively lead to the formation of confederal bodies and the increasing legitimation of truly democratic bodies. Civic banks to fund municipal enterprises and land purchases, the fostering of new ecologically oriented enterprises owned by the community, and the creation of grassroots networks in many fields of endeavor and the public weal—all these can be developed at a pace appropriate to changes being made in political life.

That capital will likely "migrate" from communities and confederations that are moving toward libertarian municipalism is a problem faced by every community, every nation, whose political life has become radicalized. Capital, in fact, normally "migrates" to areas where it can acquire high profits, irrespective of political considerations. Overwhelmed by fears of capital flight, a good case could be established for not rocking the political boat at any time. More to the point, municipally owned farms and enterprises could provide new ecologically valuable and health-nourishing products to a public becoming increasingly aware of the low-quality goods and staples being foisted on it now.

Libertarian municipalism is a politics that can excite the public imagination, appropriate for a movement direly in need of a sense of direction and purpose. Libertarian municipalism offers ideas, ways, and means not only to undo the present social order but to remake it drastically, expanding its residual democratic traditions into a rational and ecological society.

Thus, libertarian municipalism is not merely an effort simply to take over city councils to construct a more environmentally friendly city government. Such an approach, in effect, views the civic structures that exist now and essentially (all rhetoric to the contrary aside) takes them as they exist. Libertarian municipalism, by contrast, is an effort to transform and democratize city governments, to root them in popular assemblies, to knit them together along confederal lines, to appropriate a regional economy along confederal and municipal lines.

In fact, libertarian municipalism gains its life and its integrity precisely from the dialectical tension it proposes between the nation-state and the municipal confederation. Its "law of life," to use an old Marxian term, consists precisely in its struggle with the state. The tension between municipal confederations and the state must be clear and uncompromising. Since these confederations would exist primarily in opposition to statecraft, they cannot be compromised by state, provincial, or national elections, much less achieved by these means. Libertarian municipalism is formed by its struggle with the state, strengthened by this struggle, indeed, defined by this struggle. Divested of this dialectical tension with the state, libertarian municipalism becomes little more than "sewer socialism."

Many comrades who are prepared to one day do battle with the cosmic forces of capitalism find that libertarian municipalism is too thorny, irrelevant, or vague and opt instead for what is basically a form of political particularism. Such radicals may choose to brush libertarian municipalism aside as "a ludicrous tactic," but it never ceases to amaze me that revolutionaries who are committed to the "overthrow" of capitalism find it too difficult to function politically, including electorally, in their own neighborhoods for a new politics based on a genuine democracy. If they cannot provide a transformative politics for their own neighborhood—a relatively modest task—or diligently work at doing so with the constancy that used to mark the left movements of the past, I find it very hard to believe that they will ever do much harm to the present social system. Indeed, by creating cultural centers, parks, and good housing, they may well be improving the system by giving capitalism a human face without diminishing its underlying "unfreedom" as a hierarchical and class society.

A range of struggles for "identity" has often fractured rising radical movements since SDS in the 1960s, ranging from foreign to domestic nationalisms. Because these identity struggles are so popular today, some critics of libertarian municipalism invoke "public opinion" against it. But when has it been the task of revolutionaries to surrender to public opinion—not even the public opinion of the oppressed, whose views can often be very reactionary? Truth has its own life, regardless of whether the oppressed masses perceive or agree on what is true. Nor is it elitist to invoke truth, in contradiction to even radical public opinion, when that opinion essentially seeks a march backward into the politics of particularism and even racism. We must challenge the existing society on behalf of our shared common humanity, not on the basis of gender, race, age, and the like.

Critics of libertarian municipalism dispute even the very possibility of a "general interest." If the face-to-face democracy advocated by libertarian municipalism and the need to extend the premises of democracy beyond mere justice to complete freedom do not suffice as a general interest, it would seem to me that the need to repair our relationship with the natural world is certainly a general interest that is beyond dispute—and it remains the general interest advanced by social ecology. It may be possible to co-opt many dissatisfied elements in the present society, but nature is not co-optable. Indeed, the only politics that remains for the Left is one based on the premise that there is a "general interest" in democratizing society and preserving the planet. Now that traditional forces such as the workers' movement have ebbed from the historical scene, it can be said with almost complete certainty that without a politics akin to libertarian municipalism, the Left will have no politics whatever. A dialectical view of the relationship of confederalism to the nation-state; an understanding of the narrowness, introverted character, and parochialism of identity movements; and a recognition that the workers' movement is essentially dead—all illustrate that if a new politics is going to develop today, it must be unflinchingly public, in contrast to the alternative café "politics" advanced by many radicals today. It must be electoral on a municipal basis, confederal in its vision, and revolutionary in its character.

Indeed, confederal libertarian municipalism is precisely the "Commune of communes" for which anarchists have fought over the past two centuries. Today, it is the "red button" that must be pushed if a radical movement is to open the door to the public sphere. To leave that button untouched and slip back into the worst habits of the post-1968 New Left, when the notion of "power" was divested of utopian or imaginative qualities, is to reduce radicalism to yet another subculture that will probably live more on heroic memories than on the hopes of a rational future.

October 1991

6

Cities: The Unfolding of Reason in History

Libertarian municipalism constitutes the politics of social ecology, a revolutionary effort in which freedom is given institutional form in public assemblies that become decision-making bodies. It depends upon libertarian leftists running candidates at the local municipal level, calling for the division of municipalities into wards, where popular assemblies can be created that bring people into full and direct participation in political life. Having democratized themselves, municipalities would confederate into a dual power to oppose the nation-state and ultimately dispense with it and with the economic forces that underpin statism as such. Libertarian municipalism is thus both a historical goal and a concordant means to achieve the revolutionary "Commune of communes."

Libertarian municipalism is above all a *politics* that seeks to create a vital democratic public sphere. In *From Urbanization to Cities*, as well as other works, I have made careful but crucial distinctions between three societal realms: the social, the political, and the state. What people do in their homes, what friendships they form, the communal lifestyles they practice, the way they make their living, their sexual behavior, the cultural artifacts they consume, and the rapture and ecstasy they experience on mountaintops—all these personal as well as materially necessary activities belong to what I call the *social* sphere of life. Families, friends, and communal living arrangements are part of the social realm. Apart from matters of human rights, it is the business of no one to sit in judgment of what consenting adults freely engage in sexually, the hobbies they prefer, the kinds of friends they adopt, or the spiritual practices they may choose to perform. However much these aspects of life interact with one another, none of these *social* aspects of human life properly belongs to the *public* sphere, which I explicitly identify with *politics* in the Hellenic sense of the term. In creating a new politics based on social ecology, we are concerned with what people do in this public or political sphere.

Libertarian municipalism is not a substitute for the manifold dimensions of cultural or even private life. Yet, once individuals leave the social realm and enter the public sphere, it is precisely the municipality that they must deal with directly. Doubtless the municipality is usually the place where even a great deal of social life is existentially lived—school, work, entertainment, and simple pleasures like walking, bicycling, and disporting themselves—which does not efface its distinctiveness as a unique sphere of life. As a project for entering into the public sphere, libertarian municipalism calls for a radical presence in a community that addresses the question of who shall exercise power in a lived sense; indeed, it is truly a political culture that seeks to reempower the individual and sharpen his or her sensibility as a living citizen.

Today, the concept of citizenship has already undergone serious erosion through the reduction of citizens to "constituents" of statist jurisdictions, or to "taxpayers" who sustain statist institutions. To further reduce citizenship to "personhood"—or to etherealize the concept by speaking of an airy "earth citizenship"—is nothing short of reactionary. It took long millennia for history to create the concept of the citizen as a self-managing and competent agent in democratically shaping a polity. During the French Revolution, the term *citoyen* was used precisely to efface the status-generated relegation of individuals to mere "subjects" of the Bourbon kings. Moreover, revolutionaries of the last century, from Marx to Bakunin, referred to themselves as "citizens" long before the appellation "comrade" replaced it.

We must not lose sight of the fact that the citizen culminates the transformation of ethnic tribal folk—societies structured around biological facts like kinship, gender differences, and age groups—into a secular, rational, and humane community. Indeed, much of the National Socialist war against "Jewish cosmopolitanism" was in fact an ethnically (*völkisch*) nationalistic war against the Enlightenment ideal of the *citoyen*. For it was precisely the depoliticized, indeed, animalized "loyal subject" rather than the citizen that the Nazis incorporated into their racial image of the German *Volk*, the abject, status-defined creature of Hitler's hierarchical *Führerprinzip*. Once citizenship becomes contentless through the deflation of its existential political reality or, equally treacherously, by the expansion of its historic development into a "planetary" metaphor, we have come a long way toward accepting the barbarism that the capitalist system is now fostering with certain Heideggerian versions of ecology.

To those who level the complaint against libertarian municipalism that the Greek polis was marred by "the exclusion of women, slaves, and foreigners," I would say that we must always remember that libertarian municipalists are also libertarian communists, who obviously oppose hierarchy, including patriarchy and chattel slavery. As it turns out, in fact, the "Greek polis" is neither an ideal nor a model for anything, except perhaps for Rousseau, who greatly admired Sparta. It is the Athenian polis whose democratic institutions I often describe that has the greatest significance for the democratic tradition. In the context of libertarian municipalism, its significance is to provide us with evidence that a people, for a time, could quite self-consciously establish and maintain a direct democracy, despite the existence of slavery, patriarchy, economic and class inequalities, agonistic behavior, and even imperialism, all of which existed throughout the ancient Mediterranean world. The fact is that we must look for what is new and innovative in a historical period, even as we acknowledge continuities with social structures that prevailed in the past.

In fact, short of the hazy Neolithic village traditions that Marija Gimbutas, Riane Eisler, and William Irwin Thompson hypostatize, we will have a hard time finding any tradition that was not patriarchal to one degree or another. Rejecting all patriarchal societies as sources of institutional study would mean that we must abandon not only the Athenian polis but the free medieval communes and their confederations, the *Comuñero* movement of sixteenth-century Spain, the revolutionary Parisian sections of 1793, the Paris Commune of 1871, and even the Spanish anarchist collectives of 1936–37. All of these institutional developments, be it noted, were marred to one degree or another by patriarchal values.

Libertarian municipalists are not ignorant of these very real historical limitations; nor is libertarian municipalism based on any historical "models." No libertarian municipalist believes that society and cities as they exist today can suddenly be transformed into a directly democratic and rational society. The revolutionary transformation we seek is one that requires education, the formation of a movement, and the patience to cope with defeats. As I have emphasized again and again, a libertarian municipalist practice begins, minimally, with an attempt to enlarge local freedom at the expense of state power. And it does this by example, by education, and by entering the public sphere (that is, into local elections or extralegal assemblies), where ideas can be raised among ordinary people that open the possibility of a lived practice. In short, libertarian municipalism involves a vibrant politics in the real world to change society and public consciousness alike. It tries to forge a movement that will enter into open confrontation with the state and the bourgeoisie, not cravenly sneak around them.

It is important to observe that this appeal to a new politics of citizenship is not in any way meant to gloss over very real social conflicts, nor is it an appeal to class neutrality. The fact is that "the People" I invoke does not include Chase Manhattan Bank, General Motors, or any class exploiters and economic bandits. The "People" I am addressing are an oppressed humanity, all of whom must—if they are to eliminate their oppressions—try to remove the shared roots of oppression as such.

We cannot ignore class interests by completely absorbing them into transclass ones. But in our time, particularization is being over-emphasized to the point where any shared struggle must now overcome not only differences in class, gender, ethnicity, "and other issues," but nationalism, religious zealotry, and identity based on even minor distinctions in status. The role of the revolutionary movement for over two centuries has been to emphasize our *shared* humanity precisely against ruling status groups and classes, which Marx, even in singling out the proletariat as hegemonic, viewed as a "universal class." Nor are all "images" that people have of themselves as classes, genders, races, nationalities, and cultural groups rational or humane, evidence of consciousness or desirable from a radical viewpoint. In principle, there is no reason why *différance* as such should not entangle and paralyze us completely in our multifarious and self-enclosed "particularity," in postmodernist Derridean fashion. Indeed, today, when parochial differences among the oppressed have been reduced to microscopic divisions, it is all the more important for a revolutionary movement to resolutely point out the common sources of oppression as such, and the extent to which commodification has universalized them—particularly global capitalism.

The deformations of the past were created largely by the famous "social question," notably by class exploitation, which in great measure could have been remedied by technological advances. In short, they were scarcity societies, albeit not that alone. A new social-ecological sensibility has to be created, as do new values and relationships; this will be done partly by overcoming economic need, however economic need is construed. Little doubt should exist that a call for an end to economic exploitation must be a central feature in any social ecology program and movement, which are part of the Enlightenment tradition and its revolutionary outcome.

The essence of dialectic is to always search out what is new in any development: specifically, for the purposes of this discussion, the emergence of a transclass people, such as oppressed women, people of color, even the middle classes, as well as subcultures defined by sexual preferences and lifestyles. To particularize distinctions (largely created by the existing social order) to the point of reducing oppressed people to seemingly "diverse persons"—indeed, to mere "personhood"—is to feed into the current privatistic fads of our time and to remove all possibility for collective social action and revolutionary change.

To examine what is really at issue in the questions of municipalism, confederalism, and citizenship, as well as the distinction between the social and the political, we must ground these notions in a historical background where we can locate the meaning of the city (properly conceived in distinction to the megalopolis), the citizen, and the political sphere in the human condition.

Historical experience began to advance beyond a conception of mere cyclical time, trapped in the stasis of eternal recurrence, into a creative history insofar as intelligence and wisdom—more properly, reason—began to inform human affairs. Over the course of a hundred thousand years or so, *Homo sapiens* slowly overcame the sluggishness of their more animalistic cousins the Neanderthals and entered as an increasingly active agent into the surrounding world, both to meet their more complex needs (material as well as ideological), and to alter that environment by means of tools and, yes, instrumental rationality. Life became longer, more secure, increasingly acculturated aesthetically; and human communities, at different levels of their development, tried to define and resolve the problems of freedom and consciousness.

The necessary conditions for freedom and consciousness—or preconditions, as socialists of all kinds recognized in the last century and a half—involved technological advances that, in a rational society, *could* emancipate people from the immediate, animalistic concerns of self-maintenance, increase the realm of freedom from constrictions imposed upon it by preoccupations with material necessity, and place knowledge on a rational, systematic, and coherent basis to the extent that this was possible. These conditions involved humanity's self-emancipation from the overpowering theistic creations of its own imagination (creations often formulated by shamans and priests for their own self-serving ends, as well as by apologists for hierarchy), notably, mythopoesis, mysticism, antirationalism, and fears of demons and deities, calculated to produce subservience and quietism in the face of the social powers that be.

That the necessary and sufficient conditions for this emancipation have never existed in a "one-to-one" relationship with each other has provided the fuel for Cornelius Castoriadis's essays on the omnipotence of "social imaginaries," Theodor Adorno's basic nihilism, and anarcho-chaotics who, in one way or another, have debased Enlightenment ideals and classical forms of socialism and anarchism. The discovery of the spear did not produce an automatic shift from "matriarchy" to "patriarchy," nor did the discovery of the plow produce an automatic shift from "primitive communism" to private property, as evolutionary anthropologists of the nineteenth century supposed. Indeed, it cheapens any discussion of history and social change to create "one-to-one" relations between technological and cultural developments, a tragic feature of Friedrich Engels's simplification of his mentor's ideas.

In fact, social evolution is very uneven and combined. No less significantly, social evolution, like natural evolution, is profligate in producing a vast diversity of social forms and cultures, which are often incommensurable in their details. If our goal is to emphasize the vast differences that separate one society from another rather than identify the important thread of similarities that bring humanity to the point of a highly creative development, "the Aztecs, Incas, Chinese, Japanese, Mongols, Hindus, Persians, Arabs, Byzantines, and Western Europeans, plus everything that could be enumerated from other cultures" do not resemble each other, to cite the obligations Castoriadis places on what he calls "a 'rational dialectic' of history" and, implicitly, on reason itself.[20] Indeed, it is

---

20 C. Castoriadis, *Philosophy, Politics, Autonomy: Essays in Political Philosophy*, New York: Oxford University Press, 1991, 63.

unpardonable to carelessly fling these civilizations together without regard for their place in time, their social pedigrees, the extent to which they can be educed dialectically from one another, or without an explanation of *why* as well as descriptions of how they differ from each other. By focusing entirely on the peculiarity of individual cultures, one reduces the development of civilizations in an eductive sequence to the narrow nominalism that Stephen Jay Gould applied to organic evolution, even to the point where the "autonomy" so prized by Castoriadis can be dismissed as a purely subjective "norm," of no greater value in a postmodernist world of interchangeable equivalences than authoritarian "norms" of hierarchy.

But if we explore very existential developments toward freedom from toil and freedom from oppression in all its forms, we find that there *is* a history to be told of rational advances, without presupposing teleologies that predetermine that history and its tendencies. If we can give material factors their due emphasis without reducing cultural changes to strictly automatic responses to technological changes and, without locating all highly variegated societies in a nearly mystical sequence of "stages of development," then we can speak intelligibly of definite advances made by humanity out of animality; out of the timeless "eternal recurrence" of relatively stagnant cultures; out of blood, gender, and age relationships as the basis for social organization; and out of the image of the "stranger," who was not kin to other members of a community, indeed, who was "inorganic," to use Marx's term, and hence subject to arbitrary treatment beyond the reach of customary rights and duties, defined as they were by tradition rather than reason.

Important as the development of agriculture, technology, and village life were in moving toward this moment in human emancipation, the emergence of the city was of the greatest importance in freeing people from mere ethnic ties of solidarity, in bringing reason and secularity, however rudimentarily, into human affairs. For it was only by this evolution that segments of humanity could replace the tyranny of mindless custom with a definable and rationally conditioned *nomos*, in which the idea of justice could begin to replace tribalistic "blood vengeance," until later, when it was replaced by the idea of freedom. I speak of the *emergence* of the city, because although the development of the city has yet to be completed, its moments in history constitute a discernable dialectic that opened an emancipatory realm within which "strangers" and the "folk" could be reconstituted as citizens: secular and fully rational beings who in varying degrees approximate humanity's *potentiality* to become free, rational, fully individuated, and rounded.

Moreover, the city has been the originating and authentic sphere of politics in the Hellenic democratic sense of the term, and of civilization, not, as I have emphasized again and again, of the state. Which is not to say that city-states have not existed. But democracy, conceived as a face-to-face realm of policymaking, entails a commitment to the Enlightenment belief that all "ordinary" human beings are potentially competent to collectively manage their political affairs—a crucial concept in the thinking, all its limitations aside, of the Athenian democratic tradition and, more radically, of those Parisian sections of 1793 that gave equal voice to women as well as all men. At such high points of political development, in which subsequent advances often self-consciously built on and expanded more limited earlier ones, the city became more than a unique arena for human life and politics, while municipalism—*civicism*, which the French revolutionaries later identified with "patriotism"—became more than an expression of love of country. Even when Jacobin demagogues gave it chauvinistic connotations, "patriotism" in 1793 meant that the "national patrimony" was not the "property of the King of France" but that France, in effect, now belonged to *all* the people.

Over the long run, the city was conceived as the sociocultural destiny of humanity, a place where, by late Roman times, there were no "strangers" or ethnic "folk," and by the French Revolution, no custom or demonic irrationalities, but rather *citoyens* who lived in a free terrain, organized themselves into discursive assemblies, and advanced canons of secularity and *fraternité*, or more broadly, solidarity and *philia*, hopefully guided by reason. Moreover, the French revolutionary tradition was strongly confederalist until the dictatorial Jacobin Republic came into being, wiping out the Parisian sections as well as the ideal of a *fête de la fédération*. One must read Jules Michelet's account of the Great Revolution to learn the extent to which civicism was identified with municipal liberty and *fraternité* with local confederations, indeed a "republic" of confederations, between 1790 and 1793. One must explore the endeavors of Jean Varlet and the Évêché militants of May 30–31, 1793, to understand how close the Revolution came in the insurrection of June 2 to constructing the cherished confederal Commune of communes that lingered in the historical memory of the Parisian *fédérés*, as they designated themselves, in 1871.

Hence, let me stress that a libertarian municipalist politics is not a mere strategy for human emancipation; it is a rigorous and ethical concordance of means and ends (of instrumentalities, so to speak) with historic goals, which implies a concept of history as more than mere chronicles or a scattered archipelago of self-enclosed "social imaginaries."

The *civitas*, humanly scaled and democratically structured, is the potential home of a universal *humanitas*. It is the initiating arena of rational reflection, discursive decision-making, and secularity in human affairs. It speaks to us from across the centuries in Pericles' magnificent funeral oration and in the earthy, amazingly familiar and eminently secular satires of Aristophanes, whose works demolish Castoriadis's emphasis on the *mysterium* and "closure" of the Athenian polis to the modern mind. No one who reads the chronicles of Western humanity can ignore the rational dialectic that underlies the accumulation of mere events and that reveals an unfolding of the human potentiality for universality, rationality, secularity, and freedom in an eductive relationship that alone should be called *History*. This history, to the extent that it has culminations at given moments of development on which later civilizations built, is anchored in the evolution of a secular public sphere, in *politics*, in the emergence of the rational city—the city that is rational institutionally, creatively, and communally. Nor can imagination be excluded from

History, but it is an imagination that must be elucidated by reason. For nothing can be more dangerous to a society, indeed to the world today, than the kind of unbridled imagination, unguided by reason, that so easily lent itself to Nuremberg rallies, fascist demonstrations, Stalinist idolatry, and death camps.

Instead of retreating to quietism, mysticism, and purely personalized appeals for change, we must together explore the kinds of institutions that would be required in a rational, ecological society, the kind of politics we should appropriately practice, and the political movement needed to achieve such a society. Social ecology and its politics—libertarian municipalism—seeks to do just this: to institutionalize freedom and guide us to a humane and ecological future—one that will fulfill the unfilled promise of the city in history.

September 1995

7

Nationalism and the "National Question"

One of the most vexing questions that the Left faces (however one may define the Left) is the role played by nationalism in social development and by popular demands for cultural identity and political sovereignty. For the Left of the nineteenth century, nationalism was seen primarily as a European issue, involving the consolidation of nation-states in the heartland of capitalism. Only secondarily, if at all, was it seen as the anti-imperialist and presumably anticapitalist struggle that it was to become in the twentieth century.

This did not mean that the nineteenth-century Left favored imperialist depredations in the colonial world. At the turn of this century, hardly any serious radical thinker regarded the imperialist powers' attempts to quell movements for self-determination in colonial areas as a blessing. The Left scoffed at and usually denounced the arrogant claims of European powers to bring "progress" to the "barbarous" areas of the world. Marx's views of imperialism may have been equivocal, but he never lacked a genuine aversion for the afflictions that native peoples suffered at the hands of imperialists. Anarchists, in turn, were almost invariably hostile to the European claim to be the beacon of civilization for the world.

Yet if the Left universally scorned the civilizatory claims of imperialists at the end of the last century, it generally regarded nationalism as an arguable issue. The "national question," to use the traditional phrase in which such discussions were cast, was subject to serious disputes, certainly as far as tactics were involved. But by general agreement, leftists did not regard nationalism, culminating in the creation of nation-states, as the ultimate dispensation of humanity's future in a collectivist or communist society. Indeed, the single principle on which the Left of the pre–World War I and the interwar periods agreed was a belief in the shared humanity of people regardless of their membership in different cultural, ethnic, and gender groups, and their complementary affinities in a free society as rational human beings with the capacity for cooperation, a willingness to share material resources, and a fervent sense of empathy. The "Internationale," the shared anthem of social democrats, socialists, and anarchists alike up to and even after the Bolshevik revolution, ended with the stirring cry, "The 'Internationale' shall *be* the human race." The Left singled out the international proletariat as the historic agent for modern social change not by virtue of its specificity as a class or its particularity as one component in a developing capitalist society, but by virtue of its *need* to achieve universality in order to abolish class society, that is, as the class driven by necessity to remove wage slavery by abolishing enslavement as such. Capitalism had brought the historic "social question" of human exploitation to its final and most advanced form. "Tis the final conflict!" rang out the Internationale, with a sense of universalistic commitment, one that no revolutionary movement could ignore without subverting the possibilities for passing from a "prehistory" of barbarous class interest to a "true history" of a totally emancipated humanity.

Minimally, this was the shared outlook of the prewar and interwar Left, particularly of its various socialistic tendencies. The primacy the anarchists have historically given to the abolition of the state, the agency par excellence of hierarchical coercion, led directly to their denigration of the nation-state and of nationalism generally, not only because nationalism divides human beings territorially, culturally, and economically, but because it follows in the wake of the modern state and ideologically justifies it.

Of concern here is the internationalist tradition that played so pronounced a role in the Left of the nineteenth century and the first half of the twentieth, and its mutations into a highly problematical "question," particularly in Rosa Luxemburg and Lenin's writings. This is a "question" of no small importance. We have only to consider the utter confusion that surrounds it today—as a savagely bigoted nationalism subverts the internationalist tradition of the Left—to recognize its importance. The rise of nationalisms that exploit racial, religious, and traditional cultural differences between human beings, including even the most trivial linguistic and quasi-tribalistic differences, not to speak of differences in gender identity and sexual preference, marks a decivilization of humanity.

What is particularly disturbing is that the Left has not always seen nationalism as a regressive demand. The modern Left, such as it is today, all too often uncritically embraces the slogan "national liberation"—a slogan that has echoed through its ranks without regard for the basic ideal voiced in the Internationale. Calls for tribal "identity" shrilly accentuate a group's particular characteristics to garner constituencies, an effort that negates the spirit of the Internationale and the traditional internationalism of the Left. The very meaning of nationalism and the nature of its relationship to statism raises issues for which the Left is bereft of ideas, apart from appeals for "national liberation."

If present-day leftists lose all viable memory of an earlier internationalist Left—not to speak of humanity's historical emergence out of its animalistic background, its millennia-long development away from such biological facts as ethnicity, gender, and age differences toward truly social affinities based on citizenship, equality, and a universalistic sense of a common humanity—the great role assigned to reason by the Enlightenment may well be in grave doubt. Without a form of human association that can resist and hopefully go beyond nationalism in all its popular variants—whether it takes the form of a reconstituted Left, a new politics, a social libertarianism, a reawakened humanism, an ethics of complementarity—then anything that we can legitimately call civilization, indeed, the human spirit itself, may well be extinguished long before we are overwhelmed by the growing ecological crises, nuclear war, or, more generally, a cultural barbarism comparable only to the most destructive periods in history. In view of today's growing nationalism, then, few endeavors could be more important than to examine the nature of nationalism and understand the so-called "national question" as the Left in its various forms has interpreted it over the years.

A HISTORICAL OVERVIEW

The level of human development can be gauged in great part by the extent to which people recognize their shared unity. Indeed, personal freedom consists in great part of our ability to choose friends, partners, associates, and affines without regard to their biological differences. What makes us *human*, apart from our ability to reason on a high plane of generalization, consociate into mutable social institutions, work cooperatively, and develop a highly symbolic system of communication, is a shared knowledge of our *humanitas*. Goethe's memorable words, so characteristic of the Enlightenment mind, still haunt as a criterion of our humanity: "There is a degree of culture where national hatred vanishes, and where one stands to a certain extent above nations and feels the weal and woe of a neighboring people as if it happened to one's own."[21]

If Goethe established a standard of authentic humanity here—and surely one can demand more of human beings than empathy for their "own people"—early humanity was less than human by that standard. Although a lunatic element in the ecology movement once called for a "return to a Pleistocene spirituality," they would in all probability have found that "spirituality" very despiriting in reality. In prehistoric eras, marked by band and tribal social organization, human beings were, "spiritually" or otherwise, first and

---

21 Goethe, quoted in Bertram D. Wolfe, *Three Who Made a Revolution: A Biographical History*, 3rd rev. ed., New York: The Dial Press, 1961, 578.

foremost members of an immediate family, secondly, members of a band, and ultimately, members of a tribe. What determined membership in anything beyond one's given family group was an extension of the kinship tie: the people of a given tribe were socially linked to one another by real or fictive blood relationships. This "blood oath," as well as other "biological facts" like gender and age, defined one's rights, obligations, and indeed one's identity in the tribal society.

Moreover, many (perhaps most) band or tribal groups regarded only those who shared the "blood oath" with themselves as human. Indeed, a tribe often referred to itself as "*the* People," a name that expressed its exclusive claim to humanity. Other people, who were outside the magic circle of the real or mythic blood linkages of a tribe, were "strangers" and hence in some sense were not human beings. The "blood oath" and the use of the name "the People" to designate themselves often pitted a tribe against others who made the same exclusive claim to be human and to be "the People," even among peoples who shared common linguistic and cultural traits.

Tribal societies, in fact, were extremely wary of anyone who was not one of its own members. In many areas, before strangers could cross a territorial boundary, they had to submissively and patiently await an invitation from an elder or shaman of the tribe that claimed the territory before proceeding. Without hospitality, which was generally conceived as a quasi-religious virtue, any stranger risked life and limb in a tribe's territory, so that lodgings and food were usually preceded by ritual acts of trust or goodwill. The modern handshake may itself have originated as a symbolic expression that one's right hand was free of weapons.

Warfare was endemic among our prehistoric ancestors and in later native communities, notwithstanding the high, almost cultic status enjoyed by ostensibly peaceful "ecological aborigines" among white middle-class Euro-Americans today. When foraging groups overhunted the game in their accustomed territory, as often happened, they were usually more than willing to invade the area of a neighboring group and claim its resources for their own.

Commonly, after the rise of warrior sodalities, warfare acquired cultural as well as economic attributes, so victors no longer merely defeated their real or chosen "enemies" but virtually exterminated them, as witness the near-genocidal destruction of the Huron Indians by their linguistically and culturally related Iroquois cousins.

If the major empires of the ancient Middle East and Orient conquered, pacified, and subjugated many different ethnic and cultural groups, thereby making alien peoples into the abject subjects of despotic monarchies, the most important single factor to erode aboriginal parochialism was the emergence of the city. The rise of the ancient city, whether democratic as at Athens or republican as in Rome, marked a radically new social dispensation. In contrast to the family-oriented and parochial folk who had constituted the tribal and village world, Western cities were now structured increasingly around residential propinquity and shared economic interests. A "second nature," as Cicero called it, of humanistic social and cultural ties began to replace the older form of social organization based on the "first nature" of biological and blood ties, in which individuals' social roles and obligations were anchored in their family, clan, gender, and the like, rather than in associations of their own choice.

Etymologically, "politics" derives from the Greek *politika*, which connotes an actively involved citizenry that formulates the policies of a community or polis and, more often than not, routinely executes them in the course of public service. Although formal citizenship was required for participation in such politics, poleis like democratic Athens celebrated their openness to visitors, particularly to skilled craftsmen and knowledgeable merchants of other ethnic communities. In his famous funeral oration, Pericles declared,

> We throw open our city to the world, and never by alien acts exclude foreigners from any opportunity of learning or observing, although the eyes of an enemy may occasionally profit by our liberality, trusting less in system and policy than to the native spirit of our citizens; where, in education, from their very cradles by a painful discipline

seek after manliness [in Sparta], at Athens we live exactly as we please and yet are just as ready to encounter every legitimate danger.[22]

In Periclean times, Athenian liberality, to be sure, was still limited by a largely fictitious notion of the shared ancestry of its citizens, although less than it had been previously. But it is hard to ignore the fact that Plato's dialectical masterpiece, *The Republic*, occurs as a dialogue in the home of Cephalos, whose family were resident aliens in the Piraeus, the port area of Athens where most foreigners lived. Yet, in the dialogue itself, the interchange between citizen and alien is uninhibited by any status considerations.

The Roman emperor Caracalla, in time, made all freemen in the Empire "citizens" of Rome with equal juridical rights, thereby universalizing human relationships despite differences in language, ethnicity, tradition, and place of residence. Christianity, for all its failings, nonetheless celebrated the equality of all people's souls in the eyes of the deity, a heavenly "egalitarianism" that, in combination with open medieval cities, theoretically eliminated the last attributes of ancestry, ethnicity, and tradition that divided human beings from each other.

In practice, it goes without saying, these attributes still persisted, and various peoples retained parochial allegiances to their villages, localities, and even cities, countervailing the tenuous Roman and particularly Christian ideals of a universal *humanitas*. The unified medieval world was fragmented juridically into countless baronial and aristocratic sovereignties that parochialized local popular commitments to a given lord or place, often pitting culturally and ethnically related peoples against each other in other areas. The Catholic Church opposed these parochial sovereignties, not only for doctrinal reasons but in order to be able to expand papal authority over Christendom as a whole. As for secular power, wayward but strong monarchs like Henry II of England tried to impose the "king's peace" over large territorial areas, subduing warring

---

22 Thucydides, *The Peloponnesian War*, book 2, chapter 4.

nobles with varying degrees of success. Thus did pope and king work in tandem to diminish parochialism, even as they dueled with each other for control over ever-larger areas of the feudal world.

Yet authentic citizens were deeply involved in classical political activity in many places in Europe during the Middle Ages. The burghers of medieval town democracies were essentially master craftsmen. The tasks of their guilds, or richly articulated vocational fraternities, were no less moral than economic; indeed, they formed the structural basis for a genuine moral economy. Guilds not only "policed" local markets, fixing "fair prices" and assuring that the quality of their members' goods would be high, they participated in civic and religious festivals as distinct entities with their own banners, helped finance and construct public buildings, saw to the welfare of the families of deceased members, collected money for charity, and participated as militiamen in the defense of the community of which they were part. Their cities, in the best of cases, conferred freedom on runaway serfs, saw to the safety of travelers, and adamantly defended their civic liberties. The eventual differentiation of the town populations into wealthy and poor, powerful and powerless, and "nationalists" who supported the monarchy against a predatory nobility all make up a complex drama that cannot be discussed here.

At various times and places, some cities created forms of association that were neither nations nor parochial baronies. These were intercity confederations that lasted for centuries, such as the Hanseatic League; cantonal confederations like that of Switzerland; and, more briefly, attempts to achieve free city confederations like the Spanish *Comuñeros* movement in the early sixteenth century. It was not until the seventeenth century, particularly under Cromwell in England and Louis XIV in France, that centralizers of one form or another finally began to carve out lasting nations in Europe.

Nation-states, let me emphasize, are *states*, not only nations. Establishing them means vesting power in a centralized, professional, bureaucratic apparatus that exercises a social monopoly of organized violence, notably in the form of its armies and police. The state preempts the autonomy of localities and provinces by means of its all-powerful executive and, in republican states, its legislature, whose members are elected or appointed to represent a fixed number of "constituents." In nation-states, what used to be a citizen in a self-managed locality vanishes into an anonymous aggregation of individuals who pay a suitable amount of taxes and receive the state's "services." "Politics" in the nation-state devolves into a body of exchange relationships in which constituents generally try to get what they pay for in a "political" marketplace of goods and services. Nationalism as a form of tribalism writ large reinforces the state by providing it with the loyalty of a people of shared linguistic, ethnic, and cultural affinities, indeed, legitimizing the state by giving it a basis of seemingly all-embracing biological and traditional commonalities among the people. It was not the English people who created an England but the English monarchs and centralizing rulers, just as it was the French kings and their bureaucracies who forged the French nation.

Indeed, until state-building began to acquire new vigor in the fifteenth century, nation-states in Europe remained a novelty. Even when centralized authority based minimally on a linguistic commonality began to foster nationalism throughout Western Europe and the United States, nationalism faced a very dubious destiny. Confederalism remained a viable alternative to the nation-state well into the latter half of the nineteenth century. As late as 1871, the Paris Commune called upon all the communes of France to form a confederal dual power in opposition to the newly created Third Republic. Eventually, the nation-state won out in this complex conflict, and statism was firmly linked to nationalism. By the beginning of the twentieth century, the two were virtually indistinguishable from each other.

NATIONALISM AND THE LEFT

Radical theorists and activists on the Left dealt in very different ways with the host of historical and ethical problems that nationalism raised with respect to efforts to build a communistic, cooperative society. Historically, the earliest leftist attempts to explore nationalism as a problem obstructing the advent of a free and just society came from various anarchist theorists. Pierre-Joseph Proudhon seems never to have questioned the ideal of human solidarity, although he never denied the right of a people to cultural uniqueness and even to secede from any kind of "social contract," provided, to be sure, that no one else's rights were infringed upon. Although Proudhon detested slavery—he sarcastically observed that the American South "with Bible in hand, cultivates slavery," while the American North "is already creating a proletariat"—he formally conceded the right of the Confederacy to withdraw from the Union during the Civil War of 1861–65.[23]

More generally, Proudhon's confederalist and mutualistic views led him to oppose nationalist movements in Poland, Hungary, and Italy. His antinationalist notions were somewhat diluted by his own Francophilism, as the French socialist Jean Jaures later noted. Proudhon feared the formation of strong nation-states on or near France's borders. But he was also a product, in his own way, of the Enlightenment. Writing in 1862, he declared,

> I will never put devotion to my country before the rights of Man. If the French Government behaves unjustly to any people, I am deeply grieved and protest in every way that I can. If France is punished for the misdeeds of her leaders, I bow my head and say from the depths of my soul, "*Merito haec patimur*"—We have deserved these ills.[24]

Despite his Gallic chauvinism, the "rights of Man" remained foremost in Proudhon's mind.[25] "Do you think that it is French

---

23   P.-J. Proudhon, letter to Dulieu, December 30, 1860, *Correspondence*, vol. 10, 275, republished in S. Edwards, ed., *Selected Writings of Pierre-Joseph Proudhon*, trans. Elizabeth Frazer, Garden City, N.Y.: Anchor Books, 1969, 185.

24   P.-J. Proudhon, *La Federation et l'unite en Italie*, 1862, 122–25, in Edwards, *Selected Writings,* 188–89.

25   P.-J. Proudhon, letter to Dulieu, December 30, 1860, *Correspondence*, vol. 10, 275–76, republished in Edwards, *Selected Writings*, 185.

egoism, hatred of liberty, scorn for the Poles and Italians that cause me to mock at and mistrust this commonplace word *nationality*," he wrote to Herzen, "which is being so widely used and makes so many scoundrels and so many honest citizens talk so much nonsense? For pity's sake … do not take offense so easily. If you do, I shall have to say to you what I have been saying for six months about your friend Garibaldi: 'Of great heart but no brain.'"[26]

Mikhail Bakunin's internationalism was as emphatic as Proudhon's, although his views were also marked by a certain ambiguity. "Only that can be called a human principle which is universal and common to all men," he wrote in his internationalist vein; "and nationality separates men, therefore it is not a principle." Indeed, "There is nothing more absurd and at the same time more harmful, more deadly, for the people than to uphold the fictitious principle of nationality as the ideal of all the people's aspirations." What counted finally for Bakunin was that "Nationality is not a universal human principle." Still further,

> We should place human, universal justice above all national interests. And we should once and for all time abandon the false principle of nationality, invented of late by the despots of France, Russia, and Prussia for the purpose of crushing the sovereign principle of liberty.[27]

Yet Bakunin also declared that nationality "is a historic, local fact, which like all real and harmless facts, has the right to claim general acceptance." Not only that, but this is a "natural fact" that deserves "respect." It may have been his rhetorical proclivities that led him to

---

26 P.-J. Proudhon, letter to Alexander Herzen, April 21, 1861, *Correspondence*, vol. 11, 22–24, republished in Edwards, *Selected Writings*, 191, emphasis in the original.

27 P. Maximoff, ed., *The Political Philosophy of Bakunin: Scientific Anarchism*, New York: Free Press of Glencoe, London: Collier-Macmillan Ltd., 1953, 324–35, emphasis added.

declare himself "always sincerely the patriot of all oppressed father-lands." But he argued that the right of every nationality "to live according to its own nature" must be respected, since this "right" is "simply the corollary of the general principle of freedom."

The subtlety of Bakunin's observations should not be overlooked in the midst of this seeming self-contradiction. He defined a general principle that is human, one that is abridged or partially violated by asocial or "biological" facts that for better or worse must be taken for granted. To be a nationalist is to be less than human, but it is also inevitable insofar as individuals are products of distinctive cultural traditions, environments, and states of mind. Overshadowing the mere fact of "nationality" is the higher universal principle in which people recognize themselves as members of the same species and seek to foster their commonalities rather than their "national" distinctiveness.

Such humanistic principles were to be taken very seriously by anarchists generally and strikingly so by the largest anarchist move-ment of modern times, the Spanish anarchists. From the early 1880s up to the bloody civil war of 1936–39, the anarchist movement of Spain opposed not only statism and nationalism but even region-alism in all its forms. Despite its enormous Catalan following, the Spanish anarchists consistently raised the higher human principle of social liberation over national liberation and opposed nationalist tendencies within Spain that so often divided Basques, Catalans, Andalusians, and Galicians from one another and particularly from the Castilians, who enjoyed cultural supremacy over the country's minorities. Indeed, the word "Iberian" rather than "Spanish," which appears in the name Iberian Anarchist Federation (FAI), served to express not only a commitment to *peninsular* solidarity but an indif-ference to regional and national distinctions between Spain and Portugal. The Spanish anarchists cultivated Esperanto as a "universal" human language more enthusiastically than any major radical tendency, and "universal brotherhood" remained a lasting ideal of their movement, as it has historically in most anarchist movements up to the present day.

Prior to 1914, Marxists and the Second International generally held similar convictions, despite the burgeoning of nineteenth-century nationalism. In Marx and Engels' view, the proletariat of the world had no country; authentically unified as a class, it was destined to abolish all forms of class society. *The Communist Manifesto* ends with the ringing appeal: "Working Men of All Countries, Unite!" In the body of the work (which Bakunin translated into Russian), the authors declared, "In the national struggles of the proletarians of different countries, [Communists] point out and bring to the front the common interests of the entire proletariat, independently of all nationality."[28] And further, "The working men have no country. We cannot take away from them what they have not got."[29]

The support that Marx and Engels did lend to national liberation struggles was essentially strategic, stemming primarily from their geopolitical and economic concerns rather than from broad social principle. They vigorously championed Polish independence from Russia, for example, because they wanted to weaken the Russian empire, which in their day was the supreme counterrevolutionary power on the European continent. And they wanted to see a united Germany because a centralized, powerful nation-state would provide it with what Engels, in a letter to Karl Kautsky in 1882, called "the normal political constitution of the European bourgeoisie."

Yet the manifest similarities between the internationalist rhetoric of Marx and Engels in *The Communist Manifesto* and the internationalism of the anarchist theorists and movements should not be permitted to conceal the important differences between these two forms of socialism—differences that were to play a major role in the debates that separated them. The anarchists were in every sense *ethical* socialists who upheld universal principles of the

---

28 K. Marx, F. Engels, "Manifesto of the Communist Party," *Selected Works*, vol. 1, Moscow: Progress Publishers, 1969, 120.
29 Ibid., 124.

122

"brotherhood of man" and "fraternity,"[30] principles that Marx's "scientific socialism" disdained as mere "abstractions." In later years, even when speaking broadly of freedom and the oppressed, Marx and Engels considered the use of seemingly "inexact" words like "workers" and "toilers" to be an implicit rejection of socialism as a "science"; instead, they preferred what they considered the more scientifically rigorous word *proletariat*, which specifically referred to those who generate surplus value.

Indeed, in contrast to anarchist theorists like Proudhon, who considered the spread of capitalism and the proletarianization of preindustrial peasantry and craftspeople to be a disaster, Marx and Engels enthusiastically welcomed these developments, as well as the formation of large, centralized nation-states in which market economies could flourish. They saw them not only as desiderata in fostering economic development but, by promoting capitalism, as indispensable in creating the preconditions for socialism. Despite their support for proletarian internationalism, they derogated what they saw as "abstract" denunciations of nationalism as such or scorned them as merely "moralistic." Although internationalism in the interests of class solidarity remained a desideratum for Marx and Engels, their view implicitly stood at odds with their commitment to capitalist economic expansion with its need in the last century for centralized nation-states. They held the nation-state to be good or bad insofar as it advanced or inhibited the expansion of capital, the advance of the "productive forces," and the proletarianization of preindustrial peoples. In principle, they looked askance at the nationalist sentiments of Indians, Chinese, Africans, and the rest of the noncapitalist world, whose precapitalist social forms might impede capitalist expansion. Ireland, ironically, seems to have been an exception to this approach. Marx, Engels, and the Marxist movement as a whole acknowledged the right of the Irish to national

---

30 Despite the genderedness of these words—the product of the era in which Bakunin lived—they obviously may be interpreted as signifying humanity generally.

liberation largely for sentimental reasons and because it would produce problems for English imperialism, which commanded a world market. In the main, until such time as a socialist society could be achieved, Marxists considered the formation of large, ever-more centralized nation-states in Europe to be "historically progressive."

Given their instrumental geopolitics, it should not be surprising that as the years went by, Marx and Engels essentially supported Bismarck's attempts to unify Germany. Their express distaste for Bismarck's methods and for the landed gentry in whose interests he spoke should not be taken too seriously. They would have welcomed Germany's annexation of Denmark, and they called for the incorporation of smaller European nationalities like the Czechs and Slavs generally into a centralized Austria-Hungary, as well as the unification of Italy into a nation-state, in order to broaden the terrain of the market and the sovereignty of capitalism on the European continent.

Nor is it surprising that Marx and Engels supported Bismarck's armies in the Franco-Prussian war of 1870—despite the opposition of their closest adherents in the German Social Democratic party, Wilhelm Liebknecht and August Bebel—at least up to the point when those armies crossed the French frontier and surrounded Paris in 1871. Ironically, Marx and Engels' own arguments were to be invoked by the European Marxists who diverged from their antiwar comrades to support their respective national military efforts at the outbreak of the First World War. Prowar German Social Democrats supported the Kaiser as a bulwark against Russian "Asiatic" barbarism—seemingly in accordance with Marx and Engels' own views—while the French Socialists (as well as Kropotkin in Britain and later in Russia) invoked the tradition of their country's Great Revolution in opposition to "Prussian militarism."

Despite many widespread claims that Rosa Luxemburg was more anarchistic than a committed Marxist, she actually vigorously opposed the motivations of anarchic forms of socialism and was more of a doctrinaire Marxist than is generally realized. Her opposition to Polish nationalism and Pilsudski's Polish Socialist Party (which demanded Polish national independence) as well as her hostility toward nationalism generally, admirable and courageous as it was, rested principally not on an anarchistic belief in the "brotherhood of man" but on traditional Marxist arguments, namely, an extension of Marx and Engels' desire for unified markets and centralized states at the expense of Eastern European nationalities, albeit with a new twist.

By the turn of the century, new considerations had come to the foreground that induced Luxemburg to modify her views. Like many social democratic theorists at the time, Luxemburg shared the conviction that capitalism had passed from a progressive into a largely reactionary phase. No longer a historically progressive economic order, capitalism was now reactionary because it had fulfilled its "historical" function in advancing technology and presumably in producing a class-conscious or even revolutionary proletariat. Lenin systematized this conclusion in his work *Imperialism: The Highest Stage of Capitalism.*

Thus, both Lenin and Luxemburg logically denounced the First World War as imperialist and broke with all socialists who supported the Entente and the Central Powers, deriding them as "social patriots." Where Lenin markedly differed from Luxemburg (aside from the famous issue of his support for a centralized party organization) was on how, from a strictly "realistic" standpoint, the "national question" could be used against capitalism in an era of imperialism. To Lenin, the national struggles of economically undeveloped colonized countries for liberation from the colonial powers, including Tsarist Russia, were now inherently progressive insofar as they served to undermine the power of capital. That is to say, Lenin's support for national liberation struggles was essentially no less pragmatic than that of other Marxists, including Luxemburg herself. For imperialist Russia, appropriately characterized as a "prison of nations," Lenin advocated the unconditional right of non-Russian peoples to secede under any conditions and to form nation-states of their own. On the other hand, he maintained that non-Russian

Social Democrats in Russia's colonized countries would be obliged to advocate some kind of federal union with the "mother country" if Russian Social Democrats succeeded in achieving a proletarian revolution.

Hence, although Lenin and Luxemburg's premises were very similar, the two Marxists came to radically different conclusions about the "national question" and the correct manner of resolving it. Lenin demanded the right of Poland to establish a nation-state of its own, while Luxemburg opposed it as economically unviable and regressive. Lenin shared Marx and Engels' support for Polish independence, albeit for very different yet equally pragmatic reasons. He did not honor his own position on the right to secession during the Russian Civil War, most flagrantly in his manner of dealing with Georgia, a very distinct nation that had supported the Mensheviks until the Soviet regime forced it to accept a domestic variant of Bolshevism. Only in the last years of his life, after a Georgian Communist party took command of the state, did Lenin oppose Stalin's attempt to subordinate the Georgian *party* to the Russian—a preponderantly intraparty conflict that was of little concern to the pro-Menshevik Georgian population. Lenin did not live long enough to engage Stalin on this, and other, policies and organizational practices.

TWO APPROACHES TO THE NATIONAL QUESTION

The Marxist and Marxist-Leninist discussions on the "national question" after the First World War thus produced a highly convoluted legacy that affected the policies not only of the Old Left of the 1920s and 1930s but those of the New Left of the 1960s as well. What is important to clarify here are the radically different premises from which anarchists and Marxists viewed nationalism generally. Anarchism in the main advanced humanistic, basically ethical reasons for opposing the nation-states that fostered nationalism. Anarchists did so, to be more specific, because national distinctions tended to lead to state formation and to subvert the unity of humanity, to parochialize society, and to foster cultural particularities rather than the universality of the human condition. Marxism, as a "socialist science," eschewed such ethical "abstractions."

In contrast to the anarchist opposition to the state and to centralization, not only did Marxists support a centralized state, they insisted on the "historically progressive" nature of capitalism and a market economy, which required centralized nation-states as domestic markets and as means for removing all internal barriers to commerce that local and regional sovereignties had created. Marxists generally regarded the national aspirations of oppressed peoples as matters of political strategy that should be supported or opposed for strictly pragmatic considerations, irrespective of any broader ethical ones.

Thus, two distinct approaches to nationalism emerged within the Left. The ethical antinationalism of anarchists championed the unity of humanity, with due allowance for cultural distinctions but in flat opposition to the formation of nation-states; the Marxists supported or opposed the nationalistic demands of largely precapitalist cultures for a variety of pragmatic and geopolitical reasons. This distinction is not intended to be hard and fast; socialists in pre–World War I Austria-Hungary were strongly multinational as a result of the many different peoples who made up the prewar empire. They called for a confederal relationship between the German-speaking rulers of the empire and its largely Slavonic members, which approximated an anarchist view. Whether they would have honored their own ideals in practice any better than Lenin adhered to his own prescriptions once a "proletarian revolution" actually succeeded we will never know. The original empire had disappeared by 1918, and the ostensible libertarianism of "Austro-Hungarian Marxism," as it was called, became moot during the interwar period. To their honor, in February 1934 in Vienna, Austrian socialists, unlike any other movement apart from the Spaniards, resisted protofascist developments in bloody street fighting; the movement never regained its revolutionary élan after it was restored in 1945.

NATIONALISM AND THE SECOND WORLD WAR

The Left of the interwar period, the so-called "Old Left," viewed the fast-approaching war against Nazi Germany as a continuation of the "Great War" of 1914–18. Anti-Stalinist Marxists predicted a short-lived conflict that would terminate in proletarian revolutions even more sweeping than those of the 1917–21 period. Significantly, Trotsky staked his adherence to orthodox Marxism itself on this calculation: if the war did not end in this outcome, he proposed, nearly all the premises of orthodox Marxism would have to be examined and perhaps drastically revised. His death in 1940 precluded such a reevaluation on his own part. When the war did not conclude in international proletarian revolutions, Trotsky's supporters were hardly willing to make the sweeping reexamination that he had suggested.

Yet this reexamination was very much needed. Not only did the Second World War fail to end in proletarian revolutions in Europe, it brought an end to the entire era of revolutionary proletarian socialism and the class-oriented internationalism that had emerged in June 1848, when the Parisian working class raised barricades and red flags in support of a "social republic." Far from achieving any successful proletarian revolutions after the Second World War, the European working class failed to exhibit any semblance of internationalism during the conflict. Unlike their fathers a generation earlier, no warring troops engaged in fraternization; nor did the civilian populations exhibit any overt hostility to their political and military leaders for their conduct of the war, despite the massive destruction of cities by aerial bombers and artillery. The German army fought desperately against the Allies in the West and were prepared to defend Hitler's bunker to the end.

Above all, an elevated awareness of class distinctions and conflicts in Europe gave way to nationalism, partly in reaction to Germany's occupations of home territories, but also, and significantly, as a result of the resurgence of a crude xenophobia that verged on outright racism. What limited class-oriented movements did emerge for a while after the war, notably in France, Italy, and Greece, were easily manipulated by the Stalinists to serve Soviet interests in the Cold War. Hence, although the Second World War lasted much longer than the first, its outcome never rose to the political and social level of the 1917–21 period. In fact, world capitalism emerged from World War II stronger than it had been at any time in its history, owing principally to the state's massive intervention in economic and social affairs.

STRUGGLES FOR "NATIONAL LIBERATION"

The failure of serious radical theorists to reexamine Marxist theory in the light of these developments, as Trotsky had proposed, was followed by the precipitate decline of the Old Left; the general recognition that the proletariat was no longer a "hegemonic" class in overthrowing capitalism; the absence of a "general crisis" of capitalism; and the failure of the Soviet Union to play an internationalist role in postwar events.

What came to the foreground instead were national liberation struggles in "Third World" countries and sporadic anti-Soviet eruptions in Eastern European countries, which were largely smothered by Stalinist totalitarianism. The Left, in these instances, has often taken nationalist struggles as general "anti-imperialist" attempts to achieve "autonomy" from imperialism, and state formation as a legitimation of this "autonomy," even at the expense of a popular democracy in the colonized world.

If Marx and Engels often supported national struggles for strategic reasons, the Left in the twentieth century, both New and Old, has often elevated such support for such struggles into a mindless article of faith. The strategic "nationalisms" of Marxist-type movements largely foreclosed inquiry into what kind of society a given "national liberation" movement would likely produce, in a way that ethical socialisms like anarchism in the last century did not. It was (or if not, it should have been) a matter of the gravest concern for the Old Left in the 1920s and 1930s to inquire into what type of society Mao Tse-tung, to take a striking case in point, would establish in China if he defeated the Kuomintang, while the New Left of the 1960s should have inquired into what type of society Castro, to cite another important case, would establish in Cuba after the expulsion of Batista.

But throughout this century, when Third World national liberation movements in colonial countries have made conventional avowals of socialism and then proceeded to establish highly centralized, often brutally authoritarian states, the Left often greeted them as effective struggles against imperialist enemies. Advanced as national liberation, nationalism has often stopped short of advancing major social changes and even ignored the need to do so. Avowals of authoritarian forms of socialism have been used by national liberation movements very much the way Stalin used socialist ideologies to brutally consolidate his own dictatorship. Indeed, Marxism-Leninism has proved a remarkably effective doctrine for mobilizing national liberation struggles against imperialist powers and gaining the support of leftist radicals abroad, who saw national liberation movements as largely anti-imperialist struggles rather than observing their true social content.

Thus, despite the populist and often even anarchistic tendencies that gave rise to the European and American New Left, its essentially international focus was directed increasingly toward an uncritical support for national liberation struggles outside the Euro-American sphere, without regard for where these struggles were leading and the authoritarian nature of their leadership. As the 1960s progressed, this incredibly confused movement in fact steadily shed the anarchistic and universalistic ambience with which it had begun. After Mao's practices were elevated to an "ism" in the New Left, many young radicals adopted "Maoism" unreservedly, with grim results for the New Left as a whole. By 1969, the New Left had largely been taken over by Maoists and admirers of Fidel Castro. An utterly misleading book like *Fanshen*, which uncritically applauded Maoist activities in the Chinese countryside, was revered in the late 1960s, and many radical groups adopted what they took to be Maoist organizational practices. So heavily focused was the New Left's attention on national liberation struggles in the Third World that the Russian invasion of Czechoslovakia in 1969 hardly produced serious protest by young leftists, at least in the United States.

The 1960s also saw the emergence of yet another form of nationalism on the Left. Increasingly ethnically chauvinistic groups began to appear that ultimately inverted Euro-American claims of the alleged superiority of the white race into an equally reactionary claim to the superiority of nonwhites. Embracing the particularism into which racial politics had degenerated instead of the potential universalism of a *humanitas*, the New Left placed blacks, colonial peoples, and even totalitarian colonial nations on the top of its theoretical pyramid, endowing them with a commanding or "hegemonic" position in relation to whites, Euro-Americans, and bourgeois-democratic nations. In the 1970s, this particularistic strategy was adopted by certain feminists, who began to extol the "superiority" of women over men, indeed, to affirm an allegedly female mystical "power" and an allegedly female irrationalism over the secular rationality and scientific inquiry that were presumably the domain of all males. The term "white male" became a patently derogatory expression that was applied ecumenically to all Euro-American men, irrespective of whether they themselves were exploited and dominated by ruling classes and hierarchies.

A highly parochial "identity politics" began to emerge, even to dominate many New Leftists as new "micronationalisms." Not only do certain tendencies in such "identity" movements closely resemble those of very traditional forms of oppression like patriarchy, but identity politics also constitutes a regression from the libertarian and even general Marxian message of the Internationale and a transcendence of all "micronationalist" differentia in a truly humanistic communist society. What passes for "radical consciousness" today is shifting increasingly toward a biologically oriented emphasis on human differentiation like gender and ethnicity, not an emphasis on the need to foster human universality that was so pronounced among the anarchist writers of the last century and in *The Communist Manifesto.*

TOWARD A NEW INTERNATIONALISM

How to assess this devolution in leftist thought and the problems it raises today? I have tried to place nationalism in the larger historical context of humanity's social evolution, from the internal solidarity of the tribe, to the increasing expansiveness of urban life and the universalism advanced by the great monotheistic religions in the Middle Ages, and finally to ideals of human affinity based on reason, secularism, cooperation, and democracy in the nineteenth century. We can say with certainty that any movement that aspires to something less than these anarchist and libertarian socialist notions of the "brotherhood of man," certainly as expressed in the Internationale, falls short of the highest ideals of the Left. Indeed, from the perspective of the end of the twentieth century, we are obliged to ask for even more than what nineteenth century internationalism demanded. We are obliged to formulate an ethics of complementarity in which cultural differentia mutualistically serve to enhance human unity itself, in short, that constitute a new mosaic of vigorous cultures that *enrich* the human condition and that foster its *advance* rather than fragment and decompose it into new "nationalities" and an increasing number of nation-states.

No less significant is the need for a radical social outlook that conjoins cultural variety and the ideal of a unified humanity with an ethical concept of what a new society *should be* like—one that is universalistic in its view of humanity, cooperative in its view of human relationships on all levels of life, and egalitarian in its idea of social relations. While internationalist in their class outlook, nearly all Marxist attitudes toward the "national question" were instrumental: they were guided by expediency and opportunism, and worse, they often denigrated ideas of democracy, citizenship, and freedom as "abstract" and, presumably, "unscientific" notions. Outstanding Marxists accepted the nation-state with all its coercive power and centralistic traits, be they Marx and Engels, Luxemburg, or Lenin. Nor did these Marxists view confederalism as a desideratum. Luxemburg's writings, for example, simply take confederalism as it existed in her own time (particularly the vicissitudes of Swiss cantonalism) as exhausting all the possibilities of this political idea, without due regard for the anarchist emphasis on the need for a profound social, political, and economic democratization of the municipalities that are to confederate with each other. With few exceptions, Marxists advanced no serious critique of the nation-state and state centralization as such, an omission that, all "collectivistic" achievements aside, would have foredoomed their attempts to achieve a rational society if nothing else had.

Cultural freedom and variety, let me emphasize, should not be confused with nationalism. That specific peoples should be free to fully develop their own cultural capacities is not merely a right but a desideratum. The world will be a drab place indeed if a magnificent mosaic of different cultures does not replace the largely deculturated and homogenized world created by modern capitalism. But by the same token, the world will be completely divided and peoples will be chronically at odds with one another if their cultural differences are parochialized and if seeming "cultural differences" are rooted in biologistic notions of gender, racial, and physical superiority. Historically, there is a sense in which the national consolidation of peoples along territorial lines did produce a social sphere that was broader than the narrow kinship basis for kinship societies because it was obviously more open to strangers, just as cities tended to foster broader human affinities than tribes. But neither tribal affinities nor territorial boundaries constitute a realization of humanity's potential to achieve a full sense of commonality with rich but harmonious cultural variations. Frontiers have no place on the map of the planet, any more than they have a place on the landscape of the mind.

A socialism that is not informed by this kind of ethical outlook, with a due respect for cultural variety, cannot ignore the potential outcome of a national liberation struggle as the Old and New Lefts alike so often did. Nor can it support national liberation struggles for instrumental purposes merely as a means of "weakening" imperialism. Certainly, such a socialism cannot promote the proliferation of nation-states, much less increase the number of divisive national entities. Ironically, the success of many national liberation struggles has had the effect of creating politically independent statist regimes that are nonetheless as manipulable by the forces of international capitalism as were the old, generally obtuse imperialist ones. More often than not, Third World nations have not cast off their colonial shackles since the end of the Second World War: they have merely become domesticated and rendered highly vulnerable to the forces of international capitalism, with little more than a facade of self-determination.

Moreover, they have often used their myths of "national sovereignty" to nourish xenophobic ambitions to grab adjacent areas around them and oppress their neighbors as brutally as imperialists in their own right, such as Ghana's oppression under Nkrumah of the Togo peoples in West Africa or Milosevic's attempt to "cleanse" Muslims from Bosnia. No less regressive, such nationalisms evoke what is most sinister in a people's past: religious fundamentalism in all its forms, traditional hatreds of "foreigners," a "national unity" that overrides terrible internal social and economic inequities, and most commonly, a total disregard for human rights. The "nation" as a cultural entity is superseded by an overpowering and oppressive state apparatus. Racism commonly goes hand in hand with national liberation struggles, such as "ethnic cleansing" and wars for territorial gain, as we see most poignantly today in the Middle East, India, the Caucasus, and Eastern Europe. Nationalisms that only a generation ago might have been regarded as national liberation struggles are more clearly seen today, in the wake of the collapse of the Soviet empire, as little more than social nightmares and decivilizing blights.

Put bluntly, nationalisms are regressive atavisms that the Enlightenment tried to overcome long ago. They introject the worst features of the very empires from which oppressed peoples have tried to shake loose. Not only do they typically reproduce state machines that are as oppressive as the ones that colonial powers imposed on them, but they reinforce those machines with cultural, religious, ethnic, and xenophobic traits that are often used to foster regional and even domestic hatreds and subimperialisms. No less important, in the absence of genuine popular democracies, the sequelae of understandably anti-imperialist struggles too often include the strengthening of imperialism itself, such that the powers that have been seemingly dispossessed of their colonies can now play the state of one former colony against that of another, as witness the conflicts that ravage Africa, the Middle East, and the Indian subcontinent. These are the areas, I may add, where nuclear wars will be more likely to occur as the years go by than elsewhere in the world. The development of an Islamic nuclear bomb to countervail an Israeli one or of a Pakistani bomb to countervail an Indian one—all portend no good for the South and its conflict with the North. Indeed, the tendency for former colonies to actively seek alliances with their erstwhile imperialist rulers is now a more typical feature of North-South diplomacy than is any unity by the South against the North.

Nationalism has always been a disease that divided human from human—"abstract" as traditional Marxists may consider this notion to be—and it can never be viewed as anything more than a regression toward tribal parochialism and the fuel for intercommunal warfare. Nor have the national liberation struggles that have produced new states throughout the Third World and in Eastern Europe impaired the expansion of imperialism or eventuated in fully democratic states. That the "liberated" peoples of the Stalinist empire are less oppressed today than they were under Communist rule should not mislead us into believing that they are also free from the xenophobia that nearly all nation-states cultivate or from the cultural homogenization that capitalism and its media produce.

No left libertarian, to be sure, can oppose the right of a subjugated people to establish itself as an autonomous entity. But to oppose an oppressor is not equivalent to calling for support for everything formerly colonized nation-states do. Ethically speaking, one cannot oppose a wrong when one party commits it then support another party who commits the same wrong. The trite but pithy maxim "My enemy's enemy is not my friend" is particularly applicable to oppressed people who may be manipulated by totalitarians, religious zealots, and "ethnic cleansers." Just as an authentic ethics must be reasoned out and premised on genuine humanistic potentialities, so a libertarian socialism or anarchism must retain its ethical integrity if the voice of reason is to be heard in social affairs. In the 1960s, those who opposed American imperialism in Southeast Asia and at the same time rejected giving any support for the Communist regime in Hanoi, and those who opposed American intervention in Cuba without supporting Castroist totalitarianism, stood on a higher moral ground than the New Leftists who exercised their rebelliousness against the United States predominantly by supporting national liberation struggles without regard to the authoritarian and statist goals of those struggles. Indeed, identified with the authoritarians whom they actively supported, these New Leftists eventually grew demoralized by the absence of an ethical basis in their liberatory ideas. Today, in fact, liberatory struggles based on nationalism and statism have borne the terrifying harvest of internecine bloodletting throughout the world. Even in "liberated" states like East Germany, nationalism has found brutal expression in the rise of fascist movements, German nationalism, plans to restrict the immigration of asylum seekers, violence against "foreigners" (including victims of Nazism like gypsies), and the like. Thus, the instrumental view of nationalism that Marxists originally cultivated has left many "leftists" in a condition of moral bankruptcy.

Ethically, there are some social issues on which one must take a stand, such as white and black racism, patriarchy and matriarchy, and imperialism and Third World totalitarianism. An unswerving opposition to racism, gender oppression, and domination as such must always be paramount if an ethical socialism is to emerge from the ruins of socialism itself. But we also live in a world in which issues sometimes arise on which leftists cannot take any position at all—issues on which to take a position is to operate within the alternatives advanced by a basically irrational society and to choose the lesser of several irrationalities or evils over other irrationalities or evils. It is not a sign of political ineffectuality to reject such a choice altogether and declare that to oppose one evil with a lesser one must eventually lead to the support of the worst evil that emerges. German Social Democracy, by abetting one "lesser evil" after another during the 1920s, went from supporting liberals to conservatives to reactionaries who finally brought Hitler to power. In an irrational society, conventional wisdom and instrumentalism can produce only ever-greater irrationality, using virtue as a patina to conceal basic contradictions both in its own position and in society.

"Like the processes of life, digestion and breathing," observed Bakunin, nationality "has no right to be concerned with itself until that right is denied."[31] This was a perceptive enough statement in its day. With the explosions of barbarous nationalism in our own day and the snarling appetites of nationalists to create more and more nation-states, it is clear that "nationality" is a social pathology that must be cured if society is not to further deteriorate.

SEEKING AN ALTERNATIVE

If nationalism is regressive, what rational and humanistic alternative to it can an ethical socialism offer? There is no place in a free society for nation-states—either as nations or as states. However strong may be the impulse of specific peoples for a collective identity, reason and a concern for ethical behavior oblige us to recover the universality of the city or town and a directly democratic political culture, albeit on a higher plane than even the polis of Periclean Athens. Identity should properly be replaced by community—by a

---

31 P. Maximoff, ed., *The Political Philosophy of Bakunin: Scientific Anarchism*, 325.

shared affinity that is humanly scaled, nonhierarchical, libertarian, and open to all, irrespective of an individual's gender, ethnic traits, sexual identity, talents, or personal proclivities. Such community life can only be recovered by a new politics of libertarian municipalism: the democratization of municipalities so that they are self-managed by the people who inhabit them, and the formation of a confederation of these municipalities to constitute a counterpower to the nation-state.

The danger that democratized municipalities in a decentralized society would result in economic and cultural parochialism is very real, and it can only be precluded by a vigorous confederation of municipalities based on their material interdependence. The "self-sufficiency" of community life, even if it were possible today, would by no means guarantee a genuine grassroots democracy. The confederation of municipalities, as a medium for interaction, collaboration, and mutual aid among its municipal components, provides the sole alternative to the powerful nation-state on the one hand and the parochial town or city on the other. Fully democratic, in which the municipal deputies to confederal institutions would be subject to recall, rotation, and unrelenting public review, the confederation would constitute an extension of local liberties to the regional level, allowing for a sensitive equilibrium between locality and region in which the cultural variety of towns could flourish without turning inward toward local exclusivity. Indeed, beneficial cultural traits would also be shared within and between various confederations, along with the interchange of goods and services that make up the material means of life.

By the same token, "property" would be municipalized rather than nationalized (which merely reinforces state power with economic power), collectivized (which simply recasts private entrepreneurial rights in a "collective" form), or privatized (which facilitates the reemergence of a competitive market economy). A municipalized economy would approximate a system of usufruct based entirely on one's needs and citizenship in a community rather than one's proprietary, vocational, or professional interests. Where a municipal citizens' assembly controls economic policy, no one individual controls, much less "owns," the means of production and of life. Where confederal means of administering a region's resources coordinate the economic behavior of the whole, parochial interests would tend to give way to larger human interests and economic considerations to more democratic ones. The issues that municipalities and their confederations address would cease to range around economic self-interest; they would focus on democratic procedures and simple equity in meeting human needs.

Let there be no doubt that the technological resources that make it possible for people to choose their own lifestyles and have the free time to participate fully in a democratic politics are absolutely necessary for the libertarian, confederally organized society that I have sketched here. Even the best of ethical intentions are likely to yield to some form of oligarchy, in which differential access to the means of life will lead to elites who have more of the good things in life than other citizens do. On this score, the asceticism that some leftists promote is insidiously reactionary: not only does it ignore the freedom of people to choose their own lifestyle—the only alternative in the existing society to becoming a mindless consumer—but it subordinates human freedom as such to an almost mystical notion of the dictates of "Nature." A free ecological society—as distinguished from one regulated by an authoritarian ecological elite or by the "free market"—can only be cast in terms of an ecologically confederal form of libertarian municipalism. When at length free communes replace the nation and confederal forms of organization replaces the state, humanity will have rid itself of nationalism.

March 1993

8

Anarchism and Power in the Spanish Revolution

Today, when anarchism has become *le mot du jour* in radical circles, the differences between a society based on anarchy and one based on the principles of social ecology should be clearly distinguished. Authentic anarchism above all seeks the emancipation of individual personality from all ethical, political, and social constraints. In so doing, however, it fails to address the all-important and very concrete issue of power, which confronts all revolutionaries in a period of social upheaval. Rather than address how the people, organized into confederated popular assemblies, might capture power and create a fully developed libertarian society, anarchists conceive of power essentially as a malignant evil that must be destroyed. Proudhon, for example, once stated that he would divide and sub-divide power until it, in effect, ceased to exist. Proudhon may well have intended that government be reduced to the minimum entity that could exercise authority over the individual, but his statement perpetuates the illusion that power can actually cease to exist, a notion as absurd as the idea that gravity can be abolished.

The tragic consequences of this illusion, which has burdened anarchism from its inception, can best be understood by examining a crucial event in the Spanish Revolution of 1936. On July 21, the workers of Catalonia and especially of its capital Barcelona defeated the forces of General Francisco Franco and thereby gained complete control over one of Spain's largest and most industrialized provinces, including many important cities along the Mediterranean coast and a considerable agrarian area. Partly as the result of an indigenous libertarian tradition and partly as a result of the influence exercised by Spain's mass revolutionary-syndicalist trade union, the CNT-FAI, the Catalan proletariat proceeded to organize a huge network of defense, neighborhood, supply, and transportation committees and assemblies. Meanwhile, in the countryside, the more radical peasantry (a sizable part of the agrarian population) took over and collectivized the land. Catalonia and its population were protected against a possible counterattack by a revolutionary militia, which, notwithstanding its often archaic weapons, was sufficiently well armed to have defeated the well-trained and well-supplied rebel army and police force. The workers and peasants of Catalonia had, in effect, shattered the bourgeois state machine and created a radically new government or polity in which they themselves exercised direct control over public and economic affairs through institutions of their own making. Put in very blunt terms, they had taken power—not by simply changing the names of existing oppressive institutions but by literally destroying those old institutions and creating radically new ones whose form and substance gave the masses the right to definitively determine the operations of the economy and polity of their region.[32]

Almost as a matter of course, militant members of the CNT gave their union the authority to organize a revolutionary government and provide it with political direction. Notwithstanding their reputation for indiscipline, the majority of CNT members, or *cenetistas*,

---

32 These revolutionary syndicalists conceived the means by which they had carried out this transformation as a form of direct action. In contrast to the riots, stone throwing, and violence that many anarchists today extol as "direct action," by this term they meant well-organized and constructive activities directly involved in managing public affairs. Direct action, in their view, meant the creation of a polity, the formation of popular institutions, and the formulation and enactment of laws, regulations, and the like, which authentic anarchists regarded as an abridgment of individual "will" or "autonomy."

were libertarian syndicalists rather than anarchists; they were strongly committed to a well-structured, democratic, disciplined, and coordinated organization. In July 1936, they acted not only with a due regard for ideology but often on their own initiative to create their own libertarian forms, such as neighborhood councils and assemblies, factory assemblies, and a great variety of extremely loose committees, breaking through any predetermined molds that had been imposed upon the revolutionary movement by dogmatic ideologues.

On July 23, two days after the workers had defeated the local Francoist uprising, a Catalan regional plenum of the CNT convened in Barcelona to decide what to do with the polity the workers had placed in the union's hands. A few delegates from the militant Bajo de Llobregat region on the outskirts of the city fervently demanded that the plenum declare libertarian communism and the end of the old political and social order; that is, the workers that the CNT professed to lead were offering to give the plenum the power that they had already captured and the society their militants had in fact begun to transform.

By accepting the power that was being offered to it, the plenum would have been obliged to change the entire social order in a very considerable and strategic area of Spain that was now under the CNT's de facto control. Even if it were no more permanent than the "Paris Commune," such a step would have produced a "Barcelona Commune" of even more memorable dimensions.

But to the astonishment of many militants in the union, the plenum's members were reluctant to take this decisive measure. The Bajo de Llobregat delegates and the CNT militant Juan García Olivier, to their lasting credit, tried to get the plenum to claim the power it already possessed, but the oratory of Federica Montseny and the arguments of Diego Abad de Santillán (two CNT leaders) persuaded the plenum not to undertake this move, denouncing it as a "Bolshevik seizure of power."

The monumental nature of this error should be fully appreciated because it reveals all that is internally contradictory about anarchist ideology. By failing to distinguish between a polity and a state, the CNT leaders (guided, for the most part, by the anarchistic Abad de Santillán and Montseny) mistook a workers' government for a capitalist state, thereby rejecting political power in Catalonia at a time when it was already in their hands. By refusing to exercise the power they had already acquired, the plenum did not eliminate power as such; it merely transferred it from its own hands to those of its most treacherous "allies." The ruling classes celebrated this fatal decision and slowly, by the autumn of 1936, went on to refashion a workers' government into a "bourgeois democratic" state and open the door to an increasingly authoritarian Stalinist regime.

The historic CNT plenum, it should be emphasized, did not simply reject the power that the union's own members had won at a considerable cost in lives. Turning its back on a crucial feature of social and political life, it tried to supplant reality with a daydream, not only by rejecting the political power that the workers had already placed in the CNT's hands, but by disavowing the very legitimacy of power and condemning power as such—even in a libertarian, democratic form—as an unabated evil that must be effaced. In no instance did the plenum or the CNT's leadership give the slightest evidence that it knew what to do "after the revolution," to use the title of Abad de Santillán's utopian disquisition. The CNT, in effect, had propagated revolutions and theatrical uprisings for years; in the early 1930s, it had taken up arms again and again without the least prospect of actually being able to change Spanish society, but when at last it could finally have had a significant impact on society, it stood around with a puzzled look, orphaned by the very success of its working-class members in achieving the goals embedded in its rhetoric. This was not a failure of nerve; it was a failure of the CNT-FAI's theoretical insight into the measures it would have had to undertake to keep the power it actually had acquired, indeed, that it feared to keep (and, within the logical framework of anarchism, should never have taken) because it sought the abolition of power, not simply its acquisition by the proletariat and peasantry.

If we are to learn anything from this crucial error by the CNT leadership, it is that power cannot be abolished; it is always a feature of social and political life. Power that is not in the hands of the masses must inevitably fall into the hands of their oppressors. There is no closet in which it can be tucked away, no ritual that can make it evaporate, no realm to which it can be dispatched—and no ideology that can make it disappear with moral incantations. Radicals may try to ignore it, as the CNT leaders did in July 1936, but it will remain hidden at every meeting, lie concealed in public activities, and appear and reappear at every rally.

The truly pertinent issue that confronts anarchism is not whether power will exist but whether it will rest in the hands of an elite or in the hands of the people—and whether it will be given a form that corresponds to the most advanced libertarian ideals or be placed in the service of reaction. Rather than refuse the power offered to it by its own members, the CNT plenum should have accepted it and legitimated and approved the new institutions they had already created so that the Spanish proletariat and peasantry could retain their power economically and politically.

Instead, the tension between rhetorical claims and painful realities finally became intolerable, and in May 1937, resolute CNT workers in Barcelona were drawn into open battle with the bourgeois state in a brief but bloody war within the civil war.[33] In the end, the bourgeois state suppressed the last major uprising of the syndicalist movement, butchering hundreds if not thousands of CNT militants. How many were killed will never be known, but we do know that the internally contradictory ideology called anarchosyndicalism lost the greater part of the following it had possessed in the summer of 1936.

---

33   In the intervening year, the CNT leaders had discovered that their rejection of power for the Catalan proletariat and peasantry did not include a rejection of power for themselves as individuals. Several CNT-FAI leaders actually agreed to participate in the bourgeois state as ministers and were holding office when their members were being suppressed in the battle of Barcelona in May 1937.

Social revolutionaries, far from removing the problem of power from their field of vision, must address the problem of how to give power a concrete and emancipatory institutional form. To be silent on this question, and to hide behind superannuated ideologies that are irrelevant to our present-day overheated capitalist development, is merely to play at revolution, even to mock the memory of the countless militants who have given their all to achieve it.

November 2002

9

The Future of the Left

By the beginning of the twentieth century, the Left envisioned itself as having reached an extraordinary degree of conceptual sophistication and organizational maturity. Generally, what was called leftism at that time was socialist, influenced to varying degrees by the works of Karl Marx. This was especially the case in Central Europe, but socialism was also intermixed with populist ideas in Eastern Europe and with syndicalism in France, Spain, and Latin America. In the United States, all of these ideas were melded together, for example, in Eugene V. Debs's Socialist Party and in the Industrial Workers of the World (IWW).

On the eve of World War I, leftist ideas and movements had become so advanced that they seemed positioned to seriously challenge the existence of capitalism, indeed, of class society as such. The words from the "Internationale," "Tis the final conflict," acquired a new concreteness and immediacy. Capitalism seemed faced with an insurgency by the world's exploited classes, particularly the industrial proletariat. Indeed, given the scope of the Second International and the growth of revolutionary movements in the West, capitalism appeared to be facing an unprecedented, international social upheaval. Many revolutionaries were convinced that a politically mature and well-organized proletariat could finally take conscious control over social life and evolution to satisfy, not the particularized elitist interests of a propertied minority class, but the general interests of the majority.

The "Great War," as it was called, actually did end amid socialistic revolutions. Russia established a "proletarian dictatorship," premised ostensibly on revolutionary Marxist principles. Germany, with the largest and most ideologically advanced industrial proletariat in Europe, went through three years of Marxist-influenced revolutionary upheaval, while Bavaria, Hungary, and other places experienced short-lived insurgencies. In Italy and Spain, the end of the war saw the emergence of great strike movements and near-insurrections, although they never reached a decisive revolutionary level. Even France seemed to be teetering on revolution in 1917, when entire regiments at the Western Front raised red flags and tried to make their way to Paris. Such upheavals, which recurred into the 1930s, appeared to support Lenin's view that a "moribund" capitalism had finally entered into a period of war and revolution, one that in the foreseeable future could end only with the establishment of a socialist or communist society.

By this time, moreover, major intellectual innovators, from Diderot and Rousseau through Hegel and Marx to an assortment of libertarian rebels, had brought secular and radical ideologies to a point where, sorted into a logical whole, they provided the framework for a truly coherent body of ideas that gave a rational meaning to historical development, combining a due recognition of humanity's material needs with its hopes for intellectual and social emancipation. For the first time, it seemed, without recourse to divine or other archaic nonhuman forms of intervention, humanity would finally be able to draw upon its own advancing intellectuality, knowledge, virtues, and unique capacity for innovation, to create a new world in which all the conditions would exist to actualize its potentiality for freedom and creativity. These eminently human goals, embodied in Marx's great theoretical synthesis of the ideas he had drawn from the Enlightenment as well as new ideas he had developed on his own, could be initiated in practice by the downtrodden themselves, who would be driven inexorably by the

contradictions of capitalist society into revolution and the establishment of a rational society for humanity as a whole.

I should note that many of my own words—"inexorably," "moribund," "decaying," and "general interests"—are drawn from the
literature of early twentieth-century leftist theorists and movements.
Yet, whatever may be the limits of this literature and its writers—as
we, in the new millennium, are now privileged to see in retro-
spect—this sweeping language was not the product of mere
sloganeering; it was derived from an integrated and coherent leftist
outlook and culture that appeared on the eve of the Great War. This
outlook and culture formed what we can properly call a classical
body of universalist ideas, continually enlarged by the generations
that followed the French Revolution of 1789 to 1794. In the years
that passed, this body of ideas was steadily enlarged by experience
and succeeded in mobilizing millions of people into international
movements for human emancipation and social reconstruction.

Quite obviously, the Enlightenment goals and Lenin's prognoses,
with their promise of successful socialist revolutions, were not to be
realized in the twentieth century. Indeed, what has occurred since
the midpoint of the twentieth century is a very different development: a period of cultural and theoretical decadence so far as
revolutionary ideas and movements are concerned; a period of
decomposition, in fact, that has swept up nearly all the philosophical, cultural, ethical, and social standards that the Enlightenment
had produced. For many young people who professed to hold a
radical outlook in the 1960s and 1970s, leftist theory has shriveled
in scope and content to the level of spectatorial aesthetics, often
focused on the scattered works of people like the indecisive critic
Walter Benjamin, the postmodernist Jacques Derrida, or the con-
stipated structuralist Louis Althusser, as social theory has retreated
from the lusty debating forums of 1930s socialism to the cloistered
seminar rooms of contemporary universities.

Now that the twentieth century has come to a close, we are
justified in asking, Why has humanity's emancipation failed to
achieve fruition? Why, in particular, has the proletariat failed to

make its predicted revolution? Indeed, why did the once-radical Social Democrats fail from their very inception to achieve even a majority vote in centers such as Germany? Why did they surrender so tamely to Hitler in 1933? The German Communists, of course, were simply shunted aside after 1923, assuming they could even be taken seriously in that year, except as contrived targets for demagogic propagandistic purposes to frighten the middle classes with the menace of social disorder.

How, moreover, did capitalism manage to free itself from the "chronic economic crisis" in which it seemed hopelessly mired during the 1930s? Why, especially after World War II, did it produce advances in technics so dazzling that bourgeois society is now undergoing a permanent "Industrial Revolution" whose results are difficult to foresee? Finally, why did it come to pass that, following the profound economic and social crises of the 1930s, capitalism emerged from a second world war as a more stable and more socially entrenched order than it had ever been in the past?

None of these events, so important in the predictive calculations of revolutionary Marxists, have been adequately explained in a fundamental and historical sense, notably the progressive role that Marx assigned to capitalism in his "stages theory" of history.[34] Instead, for years, Marxists largely expended their polemical energy in throwing epithets at each other and at other labor movements for their "betrayals" without asking why Marxism was so vulnerable to betrayal in the first place. In more recent years, Marxists have tried to appropriate fragments of ideas that belong to once-despised utopian ideologies, such as Fourierism (Marcuse, to cite only one

---

34 Whether in Russia or in Germany, the conviction that "bourgeois democracy" (that is, capitalism) was a preconditional stage for leading society to socialism helped justify the reluctance of Social Democracy to lead the workers to make a proletarian revolution between 1917 and 1919. Marx's "stages theory," in effect, was not only an attempt to give an interpretation to historical development; it played a vital role in Marxist politics from the German and Russian Revolutions of 1917–21 to the Spanish Revolution of 1936–37.

example) or to other ideologies, such as syndicalism, anarchism, ecology, feminism, and communitarianism, appropriating ill-fitting ideological tenets from one or the other to refurbish their limited view of a changing bourgeois reality until what passes for Marxism today is often a pastiche of fragments patched together with planks from basically alien ideologies.

How, in short, did it come to pass that the classical era, marked by its coherence and unity in revolutionary thought and practice, gave way to a completely decadent era in which incoherence is celebrated, particularly in the name of a postmodernism that equates chaotic nihilism with freedom, self-expression, and creativity—not unlike the chaos of the marketplace itself? We can answer these questions because we now enjoy over a half-century of hindsight. What the past fifty years have shown us is that the uniquely insurgent period between 1917 and 1939 was not evidence of capitalist morbidity and decline, as Lenin surmised. Rather, it was a period of social transition. During those decades, the world was so torn by circumstantially created tensions that Lenin's view of capitalism as a dying social order seemed indeed confirmed by reality.

What this classical prognosis and its supporting theoretical corpus did not take into account were various alternative developments that faced capitalism before the outbreak of the Great War and even during the interwar period—alternatives that lay beneath the tumultuous surface of the early twentieth century. The classical Left did not consider other possible social trajectories that capitalism could have followed—and eventually did follow—that would allow for its stabilization. It not only failed to understand these new social trajectories but also failed to foresee, even faintly, the emergence of new issues that extended beyond the largely worker-oriented analysis of the classical Left.

For one thing, what makes so much of the classical revolutionary prognoses formulated by prewar and wartime socialism seem paradoxical is that the "moribund" period in which many classical leftists anchored their hopes for revolution was still not even a period of "mature" capitalism, let alone one of "dying" capitalism. The era before the Great War was one in which mass production, republican systems of government, and so-called "bourgeois-democratic" liberties were still emerging from a chrysalis of precapitalist forms of craft production and commerce, state structures ruled by royal families and courts, and economies in which ennobled landlords such as the German Junkers, British aristocrats, and Latin Grandees coexisted with a huge, technically backward peasant population. Even where most great estates were owned by bourgeois elements, as in Spain, their management of agriculture was conducted lethargically, emulating the diffident economic habits that characterized parasitic agrarian elites of a precapitalist era. Capitalism, while it was the dominant economy of the United States, Great Britain, Germany, more ambiguously France, and only marginally in other European countries, was still subordinated culturally and even structurally to elite strata, often based on kinship, that were more feudal than bourgeois, and marked by the rentier and militaristic values that distinguished a waning era.

In effect, even modern industry, while becoming central to the development of major nation-states in the early twentieth century, was still anchored in a craft-peasant social matrix. The ownership of land and of small-scale workshops, often family managed, formed the traditional features of social status in a very status-ridden world, such as in England and Germany. It is hard to recall today how low the real status of women was during the early 1900s; how degraded was the status of propertyless, often mendicant workers; how eagerly even substantial capitalists tried to marry into titled families; how feeble were elementary civil liberties in a world that acknowledged the validity of inherited privilege and the authority of monarchs; and how embattled was the industrially regimented proletariat (often removed by a generation or two from village life with its more natural life-ways) in its efforts to merely organize reformist trade unions.

The Great War, a monstrous event that was as much, if not more, the product of dynastic ambitions, military obtuseness, and the awesome authority allowed to preening monarchs as it was of economic imperialism, was not a "historical necessity." An entangled Europe, caught up in Kaiser Wilhelm II's juvenile posturing and dizzying images of German national grandeur, the blind spirit of French *revanchisme* following the country's loss of Alsace and Lorraine in 1871 to the Wilhelmine Reich, and the naïve nationalism of the masses, whose class internationalism was often more rhetorical than real—all led to a horrible form of trench warfare that should have been unendurable to any civilized people within a few months after it began, let alone for four bloody years. The Deutsche Mark, the postwar German currency and emblematic expression of German capitalism, managed to perform economic prodigies that neither Wilhelm nor Hitler's bayonets could hope to perform during the last century—so different are the alternatives that the postwar era finally revealed!

Yet, ironically, it was not the battlefront in the Great War that generated the revolutions of 1917–18; it was the rear, where hunger managed to do what the terrifying explosives, machine guns, tanks, and poison gas at the front never quite succeeded in achieving—a revolution over issues such as bread and peace (in precisely that order). It is breathtaking to consider that, after three years of constant bloodletting, mutilation, and incredible daily fear, the German strikes of January 1918 that had the pungent odor of revolution actually subsided, and the German workers remained patiently quiescent when General Ludendorff's spring and summer offensives of that year gained substantial ground from French and British troops in the West to the "greater glory" of the Reich. So much for the "revolutionary instincts" of the people, which Bakunin was wont to celebrate. It speaks volumes that, despite the horrors of the Great War, the masses went along with the conflict until it was completely unendurable materially. Such is the power of adaptation, tradition, and habit in everyday life.

Notwithstanding the Russian Revolution, the Great War came to an end without overthrowing European capitalism, let alone world capitalism. The war actually revealed that the classical tradition of socialism was very limited and, in many respects, greatly in need of repair. Understandably, Lenin and Trotsky tried to foreshorten historical development and bring about the likelihood of socialism within their own life spans, although this is less true of Luxemburg and particularly of Marx, who was far more critical of Marxism than his acolytes. Indeed, Marx was at pains to warn that it had taken centuries for feudalism to die and for capitalism to emerge, hence, Marxists should hardly expect that the bourgeoisie would be overthrown in a year, a decade, or even a generation. Trotsky was far more sanguine than Lenin in his conviction that capitalism was "moribund," "decaying," "rotting," and otherwise falling apart, and that the proletariat was growing "stronger," or "more class conscious," or "organized"—but it matters little today to dwell on his expectations and prognoses.

Nevertheless, the Great War, while not completely sweeping the historical slate clean of the feudal detritus that contributed so greatly to its outbreak, left the Western world in a cultural, moral, and political stupor. An era was clearly ending, but it was not capitalism that was faced with imminent oblivion. What was disappearing was the traditional, time-worn status and class system of a feudal past, yet without any fully developed form of capitalism to take its place. With the Great Depression, British landlordism began to enter into hard, even devastating times, but it had not completely disappeared during the 1930s. The Prussian Junkers were still in command of the German army at the beginning of the 1930s and, thanks to von Hindenburg's election as president of the German state, still enjoyed many of the privileges of an established elite early in the Hitler period. But this once-haughty stratum was eventually faced with the challenge of Hitler's *Gleichschaltung*, the process of social leveling that finally degraded the Prussian officer caste. In the end, it was the Anglo-American and Russian armies that swept the Junkers away by seizing their estates in the East and dissolving them as a socioeconomic entity. France was fighting its last battles as a middle-class republic during the mid-1930s, with Catholic reactionaries and the blooded young fascists of the Croix de Feu, who aspired to an aristocratic Gallicism led by rich and titled leaders.

Thus, the interwar decades were a stormy period of transition between a declining quasi-feudal world, already shattered but not buried, and an emerging bourgeois world, which, despite its vast economic power, had still not penetrated into every pore of society and defined the basic values of the century. In fact, the Great Depression showed that the pedestrian maxim "money isn't everything" is true when there is no money to go around. Indeed, the Depression threw much of the world, especially the United States, into a disorderly one that resembled its own hectic populist era of the 1870s and 1880s, hence the flare-up of trade unionism, violent strikes, great demonstrations, and "Red" agitation that swept over the American and European continents in the 1930s.

In this socially hyperactive but indecisive period of social tensions between the old and new, when the ruling classes as well as the dominated masses lived in murderous antipathy toward each other, history unlocked the door to revolutionary upheavals. Amid the uncertainty of a tension-filled world, the fulfillment of Marx's dream—a democratic workers' system of government—seemed achievable. As a result of the strife that existed within that interwar period, it appeared that capitalism had collapsed economically and a worldwide movement toward a democratic, possibly libertarian socialist society was achievable. But to create such a society required a highly conscious movement with an able leadership and a clear-eyed sense of purpose.

Tragically, no such movement appeared. Grossly pragmatic bureaucrats such as Friedrich Ebert and Philip Scheidemann, and pedestrian theorists such as Karl Kautsky and Rudolf Hilferding, assumed the deflated mantle of the Socialist International and set its tone up until the rise of German fascism. Shortly afterward, Stalin intervened in every potentially revolutionary situation in Europe and poisoned it to serve Russia's (and his own) interests. The prestige of the Bolshevik revolution, to which this tyrant contributed absolutely nothing and which he defamed when he came to power, was still not sufficiently sullied to allow the classical Left to create its own authentic movements and expand its vision to accord with emerging social issues that reflected changes in capitalism itself.

What must now be acknowledged is that between 1914 and 1945, capitalism was enlarging its foundations with mass manufacture and new industries, not digging its grave as Lenin and Trotsky had opined. Its status as a dominant world economy and society still lay before it in 1917, not behind it. And it would be sheer myopia not to see that capitalism is still industrializing the world—agrarian as well as urban—which is basically what the word "globalization" means. Moreover, it is still eroding the particularisms that divide human beings on the basis of nationalism, religion, and ethnicity. Most of the "fundamentalisms" and "identity politics" erupting in the world today are essentially reactions against the encroaching secularism and universalism of a business-oriented, increasingly homogenizing capitalist civilization that is slowly eating away at a deeply religious, nationalistic, and ethnic heritage. The commodity is still performing prodigies of social erosion in precapitalist cultures, be they for good or bad, such as Marx and Engels described in the first part of *The Communist Manifesto*. Where sanity and reason do not guide human affairs, to be sure, the good is nearly always polluted by the bad, and it is the function of any serious revolutionary thinker to separate the two in the hope of unearthing the rational tendency in a social development.

At the same time, capitalism is not only homogenizing old societies and remaking them in its urbanized, commodity-oriented image; it is doing the same to the planet and the biosphere in the name of "mastering" the forces of the natural world. This is precisely the "historically progressive" role that Marx and Engels assigned, in a celebratory manner, to the capitalist mode of production. How "progressive" this process of homogenization is, in fact, remains to be seen. For the present, it behooves us to examine the failure of Marxism and anarchism (arguably the two principal wings of the revolutionary tradition) to deal with the transitional nature of the twentieth century.

In the post–World War II period, the weakest elements in Marx's schema of history, class struggle, capitalist development, and political activity have been subjected to penetrating critical examination.[35] The Marxian canon to the contrary, history, viewed as a whole, cannot be reduced to economic factors as Marx tried to do in his key works, although capitalism may well be mutating *Homo sapiens* into *Homo consumerans* and fostering the tendency among masses of people to experience reality as a huge market. Marx's basic views may have provided his acolytes with the necessary or preconditional causes for social development—admittedly material or economic causes—but they failed to explain the enormous role of the efficient causes; the immediate causes, such as culture, politics, morality, juridical practices, and the like (which Marx denoted as a "superstructural") for producing social change.

Indeed, what else besides "superstructural" (particularly moral, religious, and political) factors can explain why the development of capitalism, elements of which had always existed in varying degrees in agrarian and craft economies, was arrested for thousands of years and became a major economy in only one country, England, early in the nineteenth century? Or why revolutions occur only under conditions of complete social breakdown, that is, after a vast body of massively influential superstructural belief systems (often accepted in their time as eternal realities) are shattered. Marx was not oblivious to the extent to which belief systems override bourgeois forces in precapitalist societies, especially in his discussions on

---

35   I refer here not to the conventional criticisms that were mounted against Marxism by political opponents—criticisms that emerged from the very inception of Marx's theoretical activities and the emergence of the socialist movements based in varying degrees on his ideas. Nor am I concerned with Marxist critics such as Eduard Bernstein, who mounted their critiques within the Marxist movement itself in the 1890s. Rather, I refer to the critiques that emerged with the Frankfurt School and assorted writers like Karl Korsch, who seriously challenged the many premises of Marx's philosophical and historical concepts.

the predominance of agrarian values over urban ones in his *Grundrisse*. Very significantly, Marxists were riddled by conflicts over the status of capitalism at various points in its development, especially during the early twentieth century, when the bourgeoisie faced one of the stormiest periods of its history precisely because capitalism had not fully shed the trappings of feudalism and come "completely into its own," so to speak.

How, for example, was it possible for many Marxists to insist that capitalism was in decline at a time when major technical innovations like mass manufacture, radically new forms of transportation such as the automobile, advances in electrical and electronic machines and goods, and new chemical innovations were occurring in the decade directly following the Great War? Had Marx not written, after all, that "No social order ever perishes before all the productive forces [technology] for which there is room in it have developed"?[36] Could this be said of capitalism in 1914–18 and 1939–45? Indeed, will it ever be said of the capitalist mode of production in the future? In asking these questions, I am not trying to suggest that capitalism will never produce problems that necessitate its overthrow or replacement. My purpose is, rather, to suggest that the problems that may well turn most of humanity against capitalism may not necessarily be strictly economic ones or rooted in class issues.

Arguable as Marx's productivist interpretation of social development and its future may be, it becomes a very forced and artificial, even contorted, explanation of history if it is not greatly modified by the dialectic of ideas, that is, by political and social ideology, morality and ethics, law, juridical standards, and the like. Marxism has yet to forthrightly acknowledge that these different spheres of life have their own dialectic, indeed, that they can unfold from inner forces of their own and not simply result from a productivist dialectic called the "materialist interpretation of history." Moreover,

---

36 Marx, "Preface to a Contribution of the Critique of Political Economy," in *Selected Works*, Moscow: Progress Publishers, 1969, vol. 1, 504.

it has yet to emphasize that a dialectic of ethics or religion can profoundly affect the dialectic of productive forces and production relations. Is it possible, for example, to ignore the fact that Christian theology led logically to a growing respect for individual worth and finally to radical conceptions of social freedom—a dialectic that in turn profoundly influenced social development by altering the way human beings interacted with each other and with the material world?

By the time of the French Revolution, centuries of deeply entrenched ideas on property, such as the enormous esteem that accompanied the ownership of land, were intermingling and modifying seemingly objective social forces, such as the growth of an increasingly capitalistic market. As a result, the exalted image of the independent, often self-sufficient peasant who began to emerge in the wake of the Revolution with his small bit of property and his craft-oriented village, actually inhibited capitalist economic development in France well into the nineteenth century by closing off large parts of the domestic market to commodities mass produced in the cities. The image of the French Revolution as a "bourgeois" revolution that fostered a capitalist development at home is arguably more fictitious than real, although in the long run, it created many preconditions for the rise of the industrial bourgeoisie.

In short, by educing the dialectic of history along overwhelmingly productivist lines, Marx easily deceived himself as well as his most important followers, notably Lenin and Trotsky, about capitalism's morbidity by assuming that the bourgeoisie had finally prepared all the economic preconditions for socialism and hence was ready to be replaced by socialism. What he ignored was that many of the problems, contradictions, and antagonisms he imputed almost exclusively to capitalism were, in fact, the product of lingering feudal traits that society had not shed; moreover, that the seemingly "superstructural" institutions and values that had characterized precapitalist societies played a major role in defining a seemingly predominant capitalist society that was still aborning. On this score, the anarchists were right when they called not so much for the economic improvement of the proletariat as for its moral development as vital to the formation of a free society—improvements Marxists largely brushed aside as issues that fell within the domain of "private life."

Marx and Marxism also fail us when they focus overwhelmingly on the working class, even enhancing its social weight by presumably elevating transparently petty bourgeois elements such as salaried white-collar employees to proletarian status when industrial workers are evidently declining numerically. Nor does the authentic proletariat, which assumed an almost mystical class status in the heyday of Marxism, act as though it is a uniquely hegemonic historical agent in the conflict with capitalism as a system. Nothing proved to be more misleading in the advanced industrial countries of the world than the myth that the working class, when appealed to as an economic class, could see beyond the immediate conditions of its given life-ways—the factory and bourgeois forms of distribution (exchange).[37] It consistently adopted reformist programs designed to gain higher wages, shorter working days, longer vacations, and improved working conditions until thunderous events drove it to revolutionary action, together, it should be added, with nonproletarian strata. Virtually none of the classical socialist movements, it is worth noting, appealed to the workers as people: as parents, city dwellers, brothers and sisters, and individuals trying to live decent lives in a decent environment for themselves and their offspring.

Most conventional Marxist theorists to the contrary, the worker is first of all a human being, not simply the embodiment of "social labor," definable in strictly class terms. The failure of classical socialism to make a human and civic appeal to the worker—even to seriously consider him or her as more than a class being—created a warped relationship between socialist organizations and their

---

37   All of which induced Georg Lukács to impart this hegemonic role to the "proletarian party," which mystically embodies the proletariat as a class, even when its leadership is usually predominantly petty bourgeois.

alleged "constituency." Although classical Social Democracy, especially the German Social Democrats, provided workers with a highly varied cultural life of their own, from educational activities to sports clubs, the proletariat was usually boxed into a world bounded by a concern for its most immediate material interests. Even in the pre–World War II cultural centers of the socialists, such as the *casas del pueblo* established by the Spanish Socialists, it was fed primarily on discussions of its exploitation and degradation by the capitalist system, which in any case, it experienced daily in factories and workshops. The attempt to redefine the proletariat and make it a majority of a national population lost all credibility when capitalism began to create a huge "*salariat*" of office employees, managers, salespeople, and an army of service, engineering, advertising, media, and governmental personnel who saw themselves as a new middle class, deeply invested in bourgeois property through stocks, bonds, real estate, pensions, and the like, however minor these may seem by comparison with the big bourgeoisie.

Finally, a very significant failing of Marxism when it came to building a revolutionary movement was its commitment to the statist acquisition and maintenance of parliamentary power. By the late 1870s, Marx and Engels had developed into "Red Republicans," notwithstanding Marx's encomiums to the Parisian Communards and their quasi-anarchist vision of a confederal form of government. What is often ignored is that Marx disclaimed these encomiums shortly before his death a decade later. Doubtless, Marx's vision of a republic was marked by more democratic features than any that existed in Europe and America during his lifetime. He would have favored the right to recall deputies at all levels of the state, as well as minimal bureaucracy and a militia system based on working-class recruits. But none of the institutions he attributed to a socialist state were incompatible with those of a "bourgeois-democratic" state. Not surprisingly, he believed that socialism could be voted into power in England, the United States, and the Netherlands, a list to which Engels years later added France.

In vowing that only insurrection and a complete restructuring of the state were compatible with socialism, Lenin and Luxemburg, among others (especially Trotsky), decidedly departed from Marx and Engels's political ideas in their late years. At least in trying to work within republican institutions, the early Social Democrats were more consistently Marxist than were their revolutionary critics. They viewed the German Revolution of 1918–19 as an indispensable preliminary to the creation of a republican system that would open a peaceful but, more significant, institutionally sound road to socialism. That workers' councils such as the Russian soviets and German *Räte* were more radically democratic also made them frightening as institutional measures, more akin to anarchism and certainly Bolshevism than to a parliament elected by universal suffrage. Although a younger Marx would have found a state structured around councils more to his taste, there is little to show in his later writings (apart from his flirtation with the libertarian features of the Paris Commune) that he would have "smashed the state," to use Lenin's terminology, to the point of rejecting parliamentary government.

Does this mean that anarchist precepts, spawned nearly two centuries ago, provide a substitute for Marxism?

After forty years of trying to work with this ideology, my own very considered opinion is that such a hope, which I entertained as early as the 1950s, is unrealizable. Nor do I feel that this is due only to the failings of the so-called "new anarchism," spawned in recent years by young activists. The problems raised by anarchism belong to the days of its birth, when writers like Proudhon celebrated its use as a new alternative to the emerging capitalist social order. In reality, anarchism has no coherent body of theory other than its commitment to an ahistorical conception of "personal autonomy," that is, to the self-willing, asocial ego, divested of constraints, preconditions, or limitations short of death itself. Indeed, today, many anarchists celebrate this theoretical incoherence as evidence of the highly libertarian nature of their outlook and its often dizzying, if not contradictory, respect for diversity. It is primarily by giving priority to an ideologically petrified notion of an "autonomous individual" that anarchists justify their opposition not only to the state but to any form of constraint, law, and often organization and democratic decision-making based on majority voting. All such constraints are dismissed in principle as forms of "coercion," "domination," "government," and even "tyranny"—often as though these terms were coequal and interchangeable.

Nor do anarchist theorists take cognizance of the social and historical conditions that limit or modify the ability to attain "Anarchy," which is often described as a highly personal affair or even an episodic or "ecstatic" experience. Followed to its logical conclusion, indeed to its most fundamental premises, Anarchy is essentially a moral desideratum, a "way of life," as one anarchist put it to me, independent of time or place. Anarchy, we are justified in concluding, emerges from the exercise of pure will. Presumably, when enough wills converge to "adopt" Anarchy, it will simply be like the soil that remains beneath melting snow, as one British anarchist put it. This revelatory interpretation of how Anarchy makes its appearance in the world lies at the core of the anarchist vision. Anarchy, it would appear, has always been "there," as Isaac Puente, the most important theorist of Spanish anarchism in the 1930s, put it, save that it was concealed over the ages by a historically imposed layer of institutions, entrenched experiences, and values that are typified by the state, civilization, history, and morality. Somehow, it must merely be restored from its unsullied past like a hidden geological stratum.

This summary easily explains the emphasis on primitivism and the notion of "recovery" that one so often encounters in anarchist writing. Recovery should be distinguished from the notions of discovery and innovation that modern thinking and rationalism were obliged to counterpose to the premodern belief that truth and virtue in all their aspects were already in existence but concealed by an oppressive or obfuscating historical development and culture. Anarchists could just as easily use this formulation to justify social passivity rather than protest. One had only to let the "snow" (that is, the state and civilization) melt away for Anarchy to be restored, a view that may well explain the pacifism that is so widespread among anarchists throughout the world today.

In recent years, some anarchists have singled out civilization, technics, and rationality as the greatest failings of the human condition and argue they must be replaced by a more primitive, presumably "authentic" culture that eschews all the attainments of history in order to restore humanity's primal "harmony" with itself and an almost mystical "Nature." Insofar as anarchists currently espouse this view, they have actually returned anarchism to its true home after its centuries-long meanderings through the mazes of syndicalism and other basically alien social causes. Proudhon's wistful image of the self-sufficient peasant farm or village, wisely presided over by an all-knowing paterfamilias, is finally recovered; this, I would add, at a time when the world is more interdependent and technologically sophisticated than at any other in history.

Inasmuch as anarchism emphasizes primitivism as against acculturation, recovery as against discovery, autarchy as against interdependence, and naturism as against civilization—often rooting its conceptual apparatus in a "natural," conceivably "basic" ahistorical autonomous ego, freed of the rationalism and theoretical burden of "civilization"—it in fact stands in marked contrast to the real ego, which is always located in a given temporal, technological, cultural, traditional, intellectual, and political environment. Indeed, the anarchist version of the stripped-down, indeed, vacuous, ego disturbingly resembles Homer's description of the lotus eater in the Odyssey, who, while eating the lotus fruit, slips into an indolence of forgetfulness, atemporality, and blissfulness that actually represents the very annihilation of personality and selfhood.

Historically, this "autonomous ego" became the building block that anarchists used to create various movement-type structures that often gave it a highly social and revolutionary patina. Syndicalism, to cite the most important case in point, became the architectural form in which these blocks were most commonly arranged—not as a defining foundation for an anarchist movement but as a highly unstable superstructure. When workers in the closing decades of the nineteenth century became actively involved in socialism, unionism, organization, democracy, and everyday struggles for better living and working conditions, anarchism took on the form of a radical trade unionism. This association was precarious at best. Although both shared the same libertarian ambience, syndicalism existed in sharp tension with the basic individualism that pure anarchists prized, often above—and against—all organizational institutions.

Both ideologies—Marxism and anarchism—emerged at times when industrial societies were still in their infancy and nation-states were still in the process of being formed. While Marx tried to conceptualize small-scale, often well-educated Parisian craftsmen as "proletarians," Bakunin's imagination was caught up with images of social bandits and peasant jacqueries. Both men, to be sure, contributed valuable insights to revolutionary theory, but they were revolutionaries who formulated their ideas in a socially limited time. They could hardly be expected to anticipate the problems that emerged during the hectic century that followed their deaths. A major problem facing radical social thought and action today is to determine what can be incorporated from their time into a new, highly dynamic capitalist era that has long transcended the old semifeudal world of independent peasants and craftsmen; a new era, also, that has largely discarded the textile–metal–steam engine world of the Industrial Revolution, with its burgeoning population of totally dispossessed proletarian masses. Their place has been taken in great part by technologies that can replace labor in nearly all spheres of work and provide a degree of abundance in the means of life that the most imaginative utopians of the nineteenth century could not have anticipated.

But just as advances in an irrational society always taint the most valuable of human achievements with evil, so too the Industrial Revolution has produced new problems and potential crises that call for new means to deal with them. These new means must go beyond mere protest if they are not to suffer the fate of movements such as the Luddites, who could offer little more than a return to the past by trying to destroy the technical innovations of their era. Any assessment of the revolutionary tradition immediately raises the question of the future of the Left in a social environment that is not only beset by new problems but demands new solutions. What approach can incorporate the best of the revolutionary tradition—Marxism and anarchism—in ways and forms that speak to the kind of problems that face the present? Indeed, in view of the remarkable dynamism of the twentieth century and the likelihood that changes in the new one will be even more sweeping, it now behooves us to speculate about the analyses that will explain its forthcoming development, the kind of crises it is likely to face, and the institutions, methods, and movements that can hope to render society rational and nourishing as an arena for human creativity. Above all, we must think beyond the immediate present and its proximate past by trying to anticipate problems that may lie at least a generation, if not further, beyond a highly transitory present.

What remains very contemporary in Marx's writings, even after a century and a half, is the insight they bring to the nature of capitalist development. Marx fully explored the competitive forces that inhere in the buyer-seller exchange, a relationship that, under capitalism, compels the bourgeoisie to continually expand its enterprises and operations. Ever since the capitalist economy became prevalent over a sizable area of the world, it has been guided by the competitive market imperative of "grow or die," leading to continual industrial expansion and the consolidation of competing concerns into ever-larger, quasi-monopolistic complexes. Would the process of capital concentration culminate in a worldwide economy under the tutelage of a few or of a single corporate entity, thereby terminating the process of accumulation and bringing capitalism to an end? Or would capital expansion (that is, globalization) so level market differentials that the exchange of commodities as a source of accumulation becomes impossible? These were serious topics of discussion during the heyday of classical Marxism. They remain conundrums today.

Today, we can say for certain that existing quasi-monopolistic complexes furiously accelerate the rate at which society undergoes economic and social change. Not only do firms expand at an ever-increasing pace, either annihilating or absorbing their competitors, but the commodities they produce and the resources they devour affect every corner of the planet. Globalization is not unique to modern capitalist industry and finance; the bourgeoisie has been eating its way into isolated and seemingly self-contained cultures for centuries and, either directly or indirectly, transforming them. What is unusual about present-day globalization is the scale on which it is occurring and the far-reaching impact it is having on cultures that once seemed to be insulated from modern commodity production and trade and from nation-state sovereignty. Now the presumably "quaint" traits of precapitalist peoples have been turned into marketable items to titillate Western tourists who pay exorbitant prices to enjoy a presumably "primitive" item or experience.

Marx and his followers considered this process of expanding industrialization and market relations to be a progressive feature of the capitalist "stage" of history, and they expected that it would eventually eliminate all preexisting territorial, cultural, national, and ethnic ties and replace them with class solidarity, thereby removing obstacles to the development of revolutionary internationalism. Commodification, Marx famously emphasized, turns everything solid into air. It once eliminated the economic exclusivity of guilds and other economic barriers to innovation, and it continues to corrode art, crafts, familial ties, and all the bonds of human solidarity—indeed, all the honored traditions that nourished the human spirit.

Marx saw the homogenizing effects of globalization as destructive insofar as they dissolved the meaningful relationships and sentiments that knitted society together; but his formulation was not only a critique. He also saw these effects as progressive insofar as they cleared away precapitalist and particularistic detritus. Today, radicals emphasize that the worldwide invasion of the commodity into society is overwhelmingly destructive. Capitalism (not simply globalization and corporatization) not only turns everything solid into air but replaces earlier traditions with distinctly bourgeois attributes. Implicit in Marx's remarks was the belief that globalized capitalism would provide the future with a clean slate on which to inscribe the outlines of a rational society. But as capitalism writes its message of uniquely bourgeois values, it creates potentially monstrous developments that may well undermine social life itself. It supplants traditional ties of solidarity and community with an all-pervasive greed, an appetite for wealth, a system of moral accounting focused on "the bottom line," and a heartless disregard for the desperation of the poor, aged, and physically disabled.

Not that greed and heartlessness were absent from capitalism in the past. But in an earlier time, the bourgeoisie was relatively marginal and vulnerable to the patronizing outlook of the landed nobility; preindustrial values more or less held capitalists in check. Then the market economy rendered increasingly prevalent an unbridled capitalist spirit of self-aggrandizement and unfeeling exploitation. Naked bourgeois greed and heartlessness, illuminated by the vigilance of great writers such as Balzac and Dickens, produced a wave of revulsion that swept over the people exposed to it. In past epochs, the rich were neither admired nor turned into embodiments of virtue. The honored virtue of most of the precapitalist world, rather, was not self-aggrandizement but self-sacrifice, not accumulating but giving, however much these virtues were honored in the breach.

But today, capitalism has penetrated into all aspects of life. Greed, an inordinate appetite for wealth, an accounting mentality, and a disdainful view of poverty and infirmity have become a moral pathology. Under these circumstances, bourgeois traits are the celebrated symbols of the "beautiful people" and, more subtly, of yuppified baby boomers. These values percolate into less fortunate strata of the population who, depending upon their own resources, view the fortunate with envy, even awe, and guiltily target themselves for their own lack of privilege and status as "ne'er-do-wells."

In this new embourgeoisement, the dispossessed harbor no class antagonisms toward the "rich and beautiful" (a unique juxtaposition) but rather esteem them. At present, poor and middle-class people are less likely to view the bourgeoisie with hatred than with servile admiration; they increasingly see the ability to make money and accrue wealth not as indicative of a predatory disposition and the absence of moral scruples, as was the case a few generations ago, but as evidence of innate abilities and intelligence. Newsstands and bookstores are filled with a massive literature celebrating the lifestyles, careers, personal affairs, and riches of the new wealthy, who are held up as models of achievement and success. That these "celebrities" of postmodernity bubble up from obscurity is an added asset: it suggests that the admiring but debt-burdened reader can also "make it" in a new bourgeois world. Any obscure candidate can "become a millionaire"—or a multimillionaire—merely by winning in a television game show or a lottery. The myriad millions who envy and admire the bourgeoisie no longer see its members as part of a "class"; they are rather a "meritocracy," who have become, as a result of luck and effort, winners in the lottery of life. If Americans once widely believed that anyone could become the president of the United States, the new belief holds that anyone can become a millionaire or—who knows?—one of the ten richest people in the world.

Capitalism, in turn, is increasingly assumed to be the natural state of affairs toward which history has been converging for thousands of years. Even as capitalism is achieving this splendor, we are witnessing a degree of public ignorance, fatuity, and smugness unseen since the inception of the modern world. Like fast food and quick sex, ideas and experiences simply race through the human mind, and far from being absorbed and used as building blocks for generalizations, they quickly disappear to make room for still newer and faster-moving ideas and experiences of an ever-more superficial or degraded character. Every few years, it would seem, a new generation initiates ostensibly "new causes" that were exhausted only a decade or two earlier, thereby casting into ideological oblivion invaluable lessons and knowledge that are indispensable for a radical social practice. Each new generation has a concomitantly arrogant notion that history began only when it was born; hence, all experiences from the past, even the recent past, are to be ignored. Thus, the struggle against globalization, which was fought for decades under the rubric of anti-imperialism, has been reinvented and renamed.

The problem of lost definition and specificity, of everything being turned into "air," and the disastrous loss of the memory of experiences and lessons vital to establishing a Left tradition, confronts any endeavor to create a revolutionary movement in the future. Theories and concepts lose their dimensions, their mass, their traditions, and their relevance, as a result of which they are adopted and dropped with juvenile flippancy. The chauvinistic notion of "identity," which is the byproduct of class and hierarchical society, ideologically corrodes the concept of "class," prioritizing a largely psychological distinction at the expense of a sociopolitical one. "Identity" becomes a highly personal problem with which individuals must wrestle psychologically and culturally rather than a root social problem that must be understood by and resolved through a radical social approach.

Indeed, the bourgeoisie can easily remedy such a problem by promoting ethnically discriminated employees to upper-level managers and by promoting female lieutenants in the military into majors or generals. Hence the amazing willingness that new enterprises and the media exhibit in selecting blacks and women for high spots in their operations or media presentations. Baby boomer capitalists such as Tom Peters, who season their ideas of nonhierarchical practices in business administration with dashingly anarchic traits, often regard race and gender as archaisms. Colin Powell has shown that even with an African American as chairman of the Joint Chiefs of Staff, the American military can be as deadly as it needs to be, and Oprah Winfrey has demonstrated that what Americans read or buy needs have no bearing on the race or gender of a television purveyor of those commodities.

The middle and working classes no longer think of the present society as structured around classes. Current opinion holds that the rich are deserving and the poor are not, while an incalculable number of people linger between the categories. A huge section of public opinion in the Western world tends to regard oppression and exploitation as residual abuses, not inherent features of a specific social order. The prevailing society is neither rationally analyzed nor forcefully challenged; it is prudently psychoanalyzed and politely coaxed, as though social problems emerge from erratic individual behavior. Although strident protests explode from time to time, a growing gentility is watering down the severity of social disputes and antagonisms, even among people who profess leftist views.

What is absent in this type of sporadic and eruptive opposition is an understanding of the causal continuities that only serious and, above all, rational explorations can reveal. In the so-called "Seattle rebellion" in late November and early December 1999 against the World Trade Organization, what was at issue was not the substitution of "fair trade" for "free trade," but how modern society produces the wealth of the world and distributes it. Although some militant demonstrators attempted to invoke the "injustices" of capitalism (actually, capitalism was not being peculiarly "unjust" any more than lethal bacilli are being "unfair" when they produce illness and death), far fewer of the demonstrators appeared to understand the logic of a market economy. It has been reported that during anti-WTO demonstrations, little literature was distributed that explained the basic reason for denouncing the WTO and preventing its delegates from doing their business.

Indeed, the demonstration in Seattle, like the one in Washington, DC, that followed it several months later, however well-meant, created the illusion that acts of mere disruption, which became increasingly staged, can do more than moderate the "excesses" of globalization. The Washington demonstration, in fact, was so negotiated in character that the police allowed the demonstrators to walk across a chalked line as a mere symbol of illegality and then allowed themselves to be escorted into buses as arrestees. Police spokesmen pleasantly agreed that the young demonstrators were "decent" and "socially concerned kids" who meant well, and WTO delegates tolerantly acknowledged that the demonstrators drew their attention to troubling economic and environmental problems that needed correction. Undoubtedly, the authorities expect these "socially concerned kids" to eventually grow up and become good citizens.

Rather than meaningful protests, the demonstrations were noteworthy mainly because protest of any kind is such a rarity today. The limited number of participants seemed to lack an in-depth understanding of what the WTO represented. Even to protest "capitalism" is simply to voice an opposition to an abstract noun, which in itself tells us nothing about capitalist social relations, their dynamic, their transformation into destructive social forces, the prerequisites for undoing them, and finally the alternatives that exist to replace them. Few of the demonstrators appeared to know the answers to these questions; thus, they castigated corporations and multinationals as though these are not the unavoidable outcomes of historic forces of capitalist production. Would the dangers of globalization be removed from the world if the corporations were scaled down in size? More fundamentally, could smaller enterprises ever have been prevented from developing into industrial, commercial, and financial giants that would not differ from modern multinationals?

My point is less to advance criticisms than to question the extent to which the Seattle and Washington demonstrators adequately understood the problems they were dealing with. Indeed, what is a demonstration meant to demonstrate? It must not only protest but also confront official power with popular power, even in incipient form. Demonstrations are mobilizations of sizable numbers of serious people who, in taking to the streets, intend to let the authorities know that they earnestly oppose certain actions by the powers-that-be. Reduced to such antics, they become self-deflating forms of entertainment. As such, they constitute no challenge to the authorities; indeed, where idiosyncratic behavior replaces forceful opposition, they show the public that advocates of their view are mere eccentrics who need not be taken seriously and whose cause is trivial. Without the gravitas that commands respect—and, yes, the discipline that reveals serious intentionality—demonstrations and other such manifestations are worse than useless; they harm their cause by trivializing it.

A politics of mere protest, lacking programmatic content, a proposed alternative, and a movement to give people direction and continuity, consists of little more than events, each of which has a beginning and an end but little more. The social order can live with an event or series of events and even find this praiseworthy. Worse still, such a politics lives or dies according to an agenda established by the social order it opposes. Corporations proposed the WTO; they needed worldwide participation in the Organization and, in their own way, generated the very opposition that now denounces its lack of democracy and lack of humaneness. They expected opposition, and only police amateurism in Seattle let it get slightly out of hand. It ill-becomes such an opposition to then plan to protest the nominating conventions of major political parties whose very existence many demonstrators profess to oppose. Indeed, the demonstrators, however well-meaning, legitimate the existence of the parties by calling upon them to alter their policies on international trade, as though they even have a justifiable place in a rational society.

A politics of protest is not a politics at all. It occurs within parameters set by the prevailing social system and merely responds to remediable ills, often mere symptoms, instead of challenging the social order as such. The masked anarchists who join in these events by smashing windows use the clamor of shattered glass to glamorize limited street protests with the semblance of violence and little more.

I have not made these critical remarks about the state of the Left today in order to carp against people, activities, and events, or from any generational or sectarian disdain. On the contrary, my criticisms stem from a deep sympathy for people who are sensitive to injustices and particularly for those striving to remedy them. Better to do something to end the silence of popular acquiescence than simply to perpetuate the complacency generated by a consumer-oriented society.

Nor have I presented my criticisms of Marxism and anarchism—the main players in the classical Left—in order to try to astound a new generation of activists with the grandeur of revolutionary history that they somehow must match. Again to the contrary, I have invoked the classical Left of yesteryear not only to suggest what it has to teach us but also to note its own limitations as the product of a different era and one that, for better or worse, will never return. What the classical Left has to teach us is that ideas must be systematic—coherent—if they are to be productive and understandable to people who are seriously committed to basic social change. Indeed, a future Left must show that the seemingly disparate problems of the present society are connected and stem from a common social pathology that must be removed as a totality. Moreover, no attempts to change the existing society will ever prove to be fundamental unless we understand how its problems are interconnected and how their solutions can be educed from humanity's potentialities for freedom, rationality, and self-consciousness.

By coherence, I do not mean only a methodology or a system of thinking that explores root causes, but rather that the very process of attempting to link together the various social pathologies to underlying factors and to resolve them in their totality is an ethical endeavor. To declare that humanity has a potentiality for freedom, rationality, and self-consciousness—and, significantly, that this potentiality is not being realized today—leads inexorably to the demand that every society justify its existence according to the extent to which it actualizes these norms. Any endeavor to assess a society's success in achieving freedom, rationality, and self-consciousness makes an implicit judgment. It raises the searing question of what a society "should be" within its material and cultural limits. It constitutes the realizable ideal that social development raises for all thinking people and that, up to now, has kept alive movements for the fulfillment of freedom.

Without that ideal as a continual and activating presence, no lasting movement for human liberation is possible—only sporadic protests that themselves may mask the basic irrationality of an unfree society by seeking to cosmetically remove its blemishes. By contrast, a constant awareness that a given society's irrationality is deep seated, that its serious pathologies are not isolated problems that can be cured piecemeal but must be solved by sweeping changes in the often hidden sources of crisis and suffering—that awareness alone is what can hold a movement together, give it continuity, preserve its message and organization beyond a given generation, and expand its ability to deal with new issues and developments.

Too often, ideas meant to yield a certain practice are instead transported into the academy, as fare for "enriching" a curriculum and, of course, generating jobs for the growing professoriat. Such has been the unhappy fate of Marxism, which, once an embattled and creative body of ideas, has now acquired academic respectability—to the extent that it is even regarded as worthy of study. At the same time, the routine use of the word "activist" raises problems that can be unintentionally regressive. Can there be action without insight into the nature of social ills and a theoretical understanding of the measures needed to resolve them? Can the activist even act meaningfully and effectively without drawing upon the rich body of experiences and ideas that have grown over the years and that can show us the pitfalls that lie below the surface, or the many strategies that have been tested by earlier generations?

In what likely directions is capitalist society developing in the coming century, and what are the most basic problems it is raising for humanity? Is there any special sector, class, or group in society to which we must appeal if we are to hope to create a revolutionary movement? What kind of movement and institutions must we create that will play a leading role in social change? Do we need any well-organized movement at all, or will our hoped-for changes occur spontaneously, emerging out of demonstrations around specific issues or street festivals or communitarian enterprises such as co-ops, alternative enterprises, and the like? Or do we have to build political entities, and if so, what kind? What is the relationship of a revolutionary movement to these new political entities? And how should power be situated and institutionalized in a rational society? Finally, what ethical considerations should guide us in our efforts?

Marxism failed to form an adequate picture of the worker as a many-sided human being and indeed fetishized him or her to the point of absurdity. It did not normally see workers as more than economic entities, but rather endowed them with semimystical properties as revolutionary agents, possessed of secret powers to understand their interests and a unique sensitivity to radical possibilities in the existing society. To read Rosa Luxemburg, Karl Liebknecht, Leon Trotsky, the syndicalist propagandists, and even run-of-the-mill Social Democrats is to sense that they held the socialist judgment of workers in awe and imbued them with remarkable revolutionary powers. That workers could also become fascists or reactionaries was inconceivable.

This mystification has not entirely been dispelled, but even so, we must ask, which part of society can play a leading role in radical change today? The fact is that the leveling role of Western capitalism and the increasing development of social struggles along ever-vaguer lines has opened up a vista much different from that which once hypnotized the classical Left. The technological level of the Industrial Revolution was highly labor intensive; the brutish exploitation of labor and the simplification of the work process with its consequent destruction of skills by a deadening division of labor made it possible for Marx and other theorists to single out the proletariat as the principal victim of capitalism and thus the principal engine of its demise.

Although many traditional factories are still with us, especially in the Third World, in Europe and North America they are giving way to highly skilled and differentiated systems of production. Many new strata can no longer be regarded, except in the most elastic way, as "workers" in any industrial sense. Such people are even becoming the majority of the "working class," while the industrial proletariat (contrary to Marx's expectations) is visibly becoming an ever-smaller minority of the population. For the present, at least, these workers are well paid (often receiving salaries rather than wages), consumer oriented in tastes, and far removed from a working-class outlook and a disposition to hold leftist social views.

Capitalism, in effect, is creating the bases for a populist politics—hopefully a radical and ultimately revolutionary one—that is focused on the broadening and expanding of professional opportunities, the quality of life, and a more pleasant environment. Economically, maturing capitalism can properly be descriptively divided into strata of the wealthy, the well-off, the comfortable, and the poor. Industrial wage workers in the West have more in common with salaried technicians and professionals than with underpaid unskilled workers in the service sector of fast-food restaurants and retail sales and the like, let alone with the nearly lumpenized poor. In the absence of economic crises, social disquiet may focus on fears of crime, shortcomings in public services and education, the decline of traditional values, and the like. More momentously, this populist outlook fears environmental degradation, the disappearance of open spaces, and the growing congestion of once-human-scaled communities—indeed, of community life in all its aspects.

For more than a half-century, capitalism has managed not only to avoid a chronic economic crisis of the kind Marx expected but also to control crises that potentially had a highly explosive character. As a system, capitalism is one of the most unstable economies in history and hence is always unpredictable. But equally uncertain is the traditional radical notion that it must slip with unfailing regularity into periodic crises as well as chronic ones. The general population in Europe and the United States has displayed a remarkable confidence in the operations of the economy; more than 40 per cent of U.S. families have now invested in the stock market and accept its huge swings without being swept up by panics such as those that afflicted financial markets in the past. A strictly class-oriented politics based on industrial workers has receded, and the Left now faces the imperative to create a populist politics that reaches out to "the people" as they are today, in anticipation that they can now more easily be radicalized by issues that concern their communities, their civil liberties, their overall environment, and the integrity of their supplies of food, air, and water, not simply by a focus on economic exploitation and wage issues. The importance of economic issues cannot be overstated, but especially in periods of relative well-being, a future Left will be successful only to the extent that it addresses the public as a "people" rather than as a class, a population whose disquiet has at least as much to do with freedoms, quality of life, and future well-being as it does with economic crises and material insecurity.[38]

By the same token, a future Left can hope to exercise influence only if it can mobilize people on issues that cut across class lines. From Marx's day until the 1930s, the principal victims of capitalist exploitation appeared to be workers at the point of production. The French Revolution, it was argued, allowed the peasantry to gain greater control of the land, and the democratic revolutions of the eighteenth century granted the lower middle classes a major place in all spheres of French society. But they left one class unsatisfied: the emerging industrial proletariat, which was subjected to harsh working conditions, prevented from organizing, and suffered a declining standard of living. Engels portrayed a working-class life based on the English proletariat of 1844 at the height of the first Industrial Revolution; Marx argued that the concentration of capital and the displacement of workers by machines would create insufferable misery in the factories of England and the continent. This anticapitalist vision was predicated on the belief that the

---

38 I am not trying to downplay the importance of economic issues. Quite to the contrary: only in recent times, especially since the mid-twentieth century, has capitalism's commodity economy become a commodity *society*. Commodification has now penetrated into the most intimate levels of personal and social life. In the business-ese that prevails today, almost everything is seen as a trade-off. Love itself becomes a "thing," with its own exchange value and use value, even its own price—after all, do we not "earn" the love of others by our behavior? Still, this kind of commodification is not complete; the value of love is not entirely measurable in terms of labor or supply and demand.

proletariat's material conditions of life would worsen steadily while its numbers would increase to a point where it became the majority of the population.

By the late nineteenth century, however, these predictions were already falling short, and by 1950 they were wholly discredited. What with the sophistication of machinery, the appearance of electronics, the spectacular increase in motor vehicle production, the rise of the chemical industry, and the like, the proportion of industrial workers to the population at-large was diminishing, not rising. Moreover, due in large part to the struggles of legal trade unions to improve the living conditions of the proletariat in particular, the conflict between capital and labor was being significantly muted. Marxism, then, was clearly boxed into the class relations of a historically limited period, the era of the first Industrial Revolution.

Far from becoming proletarianized or declining to a minority of the population as Marx had predicted, the middle class retained the psychology and consciousness of people who could hope for an ever-higher status. Propertyless as it may have been in reality and often cowed by the real bourgeoisie, the petty bourgeoisie was (and remains to a great extent) convinced that it has a privileged place in the market economy and entertains expectations that it can climb upward on the social ladder of the capitalist system. If anything, the working class has made sufficient gains that it expects its children, equipped with a better education than their parents, to step upward in life. Millions of small property owners invest in financial markets. Workers now describe themselves as "middle class" or, with a nuance that heightens the dignity of labor, as "working families." Combative and exclusive expressions like "workers," "toilers," and "laborers" that once implicitly hinted at the existence of class struggle are now used with increasing rarity or not at all.

The sharp lines that once distinguished a factory's accounting office from the proletariat are being blurred ideologically and eating away at working-class consciousness. Notwithstanding Marx's theory of history as an account of class struggles, with its many truths, a class is no more authentic than the consciousness with which it views reality. No worker is truly a class being, however much he is exploited, when he views social life in bourgeois terms. The bourgeoisie learned this fact quite early when it exploited ethnic, religious, gender, and craft divisions within the proletariat as a whole. Hence, the blue- or white-collar worker is a class being according to how she thinks of herself, relates to her boss, and holds expectations in life. A worker without a combative class consciousness is no more an exploited proletarian, for all practical purposes, than a policeman is an ordinary worker. Radical intellectuals' mystification of the worker has its origins in their imputation that "consciousness follows being," that is, when the worker recognizes that he is exploited and that capitalism is his social enemy.

What does this mean for a future Left? Unless capitalism unexpectedly collapses into a major chronic crisis (in which case, workers may well turn to the fascism of a Le Pen in France or the reactionism of a Buchanan in the U.S.), then the Left must focus on issues that are interclass in nature, addressing the middle as well as the working class. By the very logic of its grow-or-die imperative, capitalism may well be producing ecological crises that gravely imperil the integrity of life on this planet. The outputs of factories and the raw material industries, the destructive agricultural practices, and the consumption patterns in privileged parts of the world are simplifying the highly complex ecological ties that emerged over millions of years of natural evolution, reducing highly fertile areas to concrete landscapes, turning usable water into an increasingly degraded resource, surrounding the planet with a carbon dioxide layer that threatens to radically change the climate, and opening dangerous holes in the ozone layer. Rivers, lakes, and oceans are becoming garbage dumps for poisonous and life-inhibiting wastes. Almost every tangible component of daily life, from the food on the dinner table to substances used in the workplace, is becoming polluted with known or potentially dangerous toxicants. Cities are growing into vast, polluted, sprawling environments whose populations are larger than those of many nation-states only a few decades ago. The equatorial belt of tropical forests that surround the planet's land areas and large parts of the temperate zones are being deforested and denuded of their complex life-forms.

Yet for capitalism to desist from its mindless expansion would be for it to commit social suicide. By definition, capitalism is a competitive economy that cannot cease to expand. The problems it may be creating for humanity as a whole—problems that transcend class differences—can easily become the bases for a vast critique if current environmentalists are willing to raise their concerns to the level of a radical social analysis and organize not simply around saving a select species or around the vices of automobile manufacturers but around replacing the existing irrational economy by a rational one. The fact that the nuclear industry still exists must be seen not simply as an abuse or a matter of stupidity, for example, but as an integral part of a greater whole: the need for an industry in a competitive economy to grow and outcompete its rivals. Similarly, the successes of the chemical industry in promoting the use of toxicants in agriculture, and the growing output of the automobile and petroleum industries—all must be seen as the results of the inner workings of a deeply entrenched system. Not only workers but the public must be educated in the reality that our emerging ecological problems stem from our irrational society.

Issues such as gender discrimination, racism, and national chauvinism must be recast not only as cultural and social regressions but as evidence of the ills produced by hierarchy. A growing public awareness must be fostered in order to recognize that oppression includes not only exploitation but also domination, and that it is based not only on economic causes but on cultural particularisms that divide people according to sexual, ethnic, and similar traits. Where these issues come to the foreground in the form of patent abuses, a conscious revolutionary movement must expand their implications to show that society as it exists is basically irrational and dangerous.

Such a revolutionary movement needs a distinctive body of tactics designed to expand the scope of any issue, however reformist it may seem at first glance, steadily radicalizing it and giving it a potentially revolutionary thrust. It should make no agreement with liberals and the bourgeoisie on retaining the existing order. If the solution to a specific environmental problem seems fairly pragmatic, then the movement must regard it as a step for widening a partly open door until it can show that the entire ecological problem is systemic and expose it as such to public view. Thus, a revolutionary movement should insist not only on blocking the construction of a nuclear plant but on shutting down all nuclear plants and replacing them with alternative energy sources that enhance the environment. It should regard no limited gains as conclusive but rather must clearly link a given demand to the need for basic social change. The same strategy applies to the use of chemicals in agriculture, current agricultural methods of growing food, the manufacture of harmful means of transportation, the manufacture of dangerous household products; indeed, every item whose production and use debases the environment and degrades human values.

I have examined elsewhere the reasons why power cannot be ignored—a problem that beleaguered the Spanish anarchists. But can we conceive of a popular movement gaining power without an agency that can provide it with guidance? A revolutionary Left that seeks to advance from protest demonstrations to revolutionary demonstrations must resolutely confront the problem of organization. I speak here not of ad hoc planning groups but rather of the creation and maintenance of an organization that is enduring, structured, and broadly programmatic. Such an organization constitutes a definable entity and must be structured around lasting and formal institutions to make it operational; it must contain a responsible membership that firmly and knowledgeably adheres to its ideals; and it must advance a sweeping program for social change that can be translated into everyday practice. Although such an organization may join a coalition (or united front, as the traditional Left called it), it must not disappear into such a coalition or surrender its independence, let alone its identity. It must retain its own name at all times and be guided by its own statutes. The organization's program must be the product of a reasoned analysis of the fundamental problems that face society, their historical sources and theoretical fundaments, and the clearly visible goals that follow from the potentialities and realities for social change.

One of the greatest problems that revolutionaries in the past faced, from the English revolutionaries in the seventeenth century to the Spanish in the twentieth, was their failure to create a resolute, well-structured, and fully informed organization with which to counter their reactionary opponents. Few uprisings expand beyond the limits of a riot without the guidance of a knowledgeable leadership. The myth of the purely spontaneous revolution can be dispatched by a careful study of past uprisings (as I have attempted in my own work, the four-volume history called *The Third Revolution*). Even in self-consciously libertarian organizations, leadership always existed in the form of "influential militants," spirited men and women who constituted the nuclei around which crowds transformed street protests into outright insurrections. In his famous etching *The Revolt*, Daumier intuitively focuses on a single individual, amid other rebels, who raises the cry that brings the masses into motion. Even in seemingly "spontaneous insurrections," advanced militants, scattered throughout rebellious crowds, spurred the uncertain masses on to further action. Contrary to anarchistic myths, none of the soviets, councils, and committees that arose in Russia in 1917, Germany in 1918, and Spain in 1936 were formed simply of their own accord. Invariably, specific militants (a euphemism for leaders) took the initiative in forming them and in guiding inexperienced masses toward the adoption of a radical course of action.

Absorbed as they were with making concrete and immediate demands, few of these councils and committees had a broad overview of the social possibilities opened by the insurrections they initiated or a clear understanding of the enemies they had temporarily defeated. By contrast, the bourgeoisie and its statesmen knew only too well how to organize themselves, thanks to their considerable experience as entrepreneurs, political leaders, and military commanders. But the workers too often lacked the knowledge and experience so vital to developing such a perspective. It remains a tragic irony that insurrections not defeated outright by superior military forces often froze into immobility once they took power from their class enemies and rarely took the organizational steps necessary to retain their power. Without a theoretically trained and militant organization that had developed a broad social vision of its tasks and could offer workers practical programs for completing the revolution that they had initiated, revolutions quickly fell apart for lack of further action. Their supporters, zealous at the outset and for a brief period afterward, soon floundered, became demoralized for want of a thoroughgoing program, lost their élan, and then were crushed physically. Nowhere was this destructive process more apparent than in the German Revolution of 1918–19 and also to a great degree in the Spanish Revolution of 1936–37; mainly because the mass anarchosyndicalist union, the CNT, surrendered the power it had received from the Catalan workers in July 1936 to the bourgeoisie.

A future Left must carefully study these tragic experiences and determine how to resolve the problems of organization and power. Such an organization cannot be a conventional party, seeking a comfortable place in a parliamentary state, without losing its revolutionary élan. The Bolshevik party, structured as a top-down organization that fetishized centralization and internal party hierarchy, exemplifies how a party can merely replicate a state to become a bureaucratic and authoritarian entity.

If Marxists, when they found themselves in revolutionary situations, could not conceive of any politics that abolished the state, then the anarchists, and tragically the syndicalists who were deeply influenced by them intellectually, were so fixated on avoiding the state that they destroyed vital, self-governing revolutionary institutions. This is not the place to discuss Spanish anarchism and its rather confused anarchosyndicalist "farrago," as Chris Ealham has so aptly called it, but the CNT-FAI leadership seems to have lacked the slightest idea how to achieve a libertarian communist revolution.[39] When power was actually thrust into their trembling hands, they simply did not know what to do with it.

Every revolution, indeed, even every attempt to achieve basic social change, will always meet with resistance from elites in power. Every effort to defend a revolution will require the amassing of power—physical as well as institutional and administrative—which is to say, the creation of a government. Anarchists may call for the abolition of the state, but coercion of some kind will be necessary to prevent the bourgeois state from returning in full force with unbridled terror. For a libertarian organization to eschew, out of misplaced fear of creating a "state," taking power when it can do so with the support of the revolutionary masses is confusion at best and a total failure of nerve at worst. Perhaps the CNT-FAI actually lived in awe of the very state apparatus whose existence it was committed to abolishing. Better that such a movement gets out of the way than remain cloaked in a seemingly "radical" camouflage that makes promises to the masses that it cannot honor.

The history of the libertarian Left does suggest, however, a form of organization that is consistent with attempts to create a left libertarian society. In a confederation, seeming higher bodies play the role of administering policy decisions that are made at the base of the organization. In the end, nearly all policy decisions, especially basic ones, are made at the base of the organization by its branches or sections. Decisions made at the base move to the top and then back again in modified form to the base until, by majority vote at the base, they become policies whose implementation is undertaken by special or standing committees.

No organizational model, however, should be fetishized to the point where it flatly contradicts the imperatives of real life. Where

---

39   Ealham, C., "From the Summits to the Abyss: The Contradictions of Individualism and Collectivism in Spanish Anarchism," in *The Republic Besieged: Civil War in Spain*, eds. Preston, P. and Mackenzie, A. L., Edinburgh: Edinburgh University Press, 1996, 140. This essay is one of the most important contributions I have read to the literature on the contradictions in anarchism.

events require a measure of centralization, coordination at a confederal level may have to be tightened to implement a policy or tactic, to the extent that it is necessary and only for as long as it is necessary. A confederation can allow necessary centralization on a temporary basis, without yielding to a permanent centralized organization, only if its membership is conscious and thoroughly informed to guard against the abuses of centralization and only if the organization has structures in place to recall leaders who seem to be abusing their powers. Otherwise, we have no certainty that any libertarian practices will be honored. I have seen people who for decades were committed to libertarian practices and principles throw their ideals to the wind, and even drift into a coarse nationalism, when events appealed more to their emotions than to their minds. A libertarian organization must have in place precautions such as the right to recall by the organization's membership and the right to demand a full accounting of a confederal body's practices, but the fact remains that there is no substitute for knowledge and consciousness.

A communalist society would have to make decisions on how resources are to be acquired, produced, allocated, and distributed. Such a society must seek to prevent the restoration of capitalism and of old or new systems of privilege. It must try to achieve a degree of administrative coordination and regulation on a huge scale among communities, and decision-making must be resolute if social life of any kind is not to collapse completely.

These constraints are necessary to provide the greatest degree of freedom possible, but they will not be imposed simply by "goodwill," "mutual aid," "solidarity," or even "custom," and any notion that they will rests more on a prayer than on human experience. Material want will quickly erode any goodwill and solidarity that a successful revolution might create among the libertarian victors; hence, the need for postscarcity as a precondition for a communalist society. In the Spanish Revolution of 1936–37, many of the new society's collectives, all flying the black-and-red flag of anarchosyndicalism, entered into blatant competition with one another for raw materials, technicians, and even markets and profits. The result was that they had to be "socialized" by the CNT, that is, the trade union had to exert control to equalize the distribution of goods and the availability of costly machinery, and oblige "rich" collectives to share their wealth with poor ones. (Later this authority was taken over by the Madrid nation-state for reasons of its own.) Nor were all peasants eager to join collectives when they were also afforded the opportunity to function as small property owners. Still others left the collectives in sizable numbers when they found themselves free to do so without fear. In other words, to establish a viable communalist society, more than personal and moral commitments will be needed—least of all, those extremely precarious variables that are based on "human nature" and "instincts for mutual aid."

The problem of achieving libertarian communism is one of the most untheorized aspects of the libertarian repertoire. The communist maxim "From each according to ability, to each according to need" presupposes a sufficiency of goods and hence complex technological development. That achievement involves a close agreement with Marx's emphasis that advances in the instruments of production are a precondition for communism. The success of libertarian communism, then, depends profoundly on the growth of the productive forces over many centuries and on the increasing availability of the means of life.

History is filled with countless examples where natural scarcity or limited resources obliged peoples to turn popular governments into kingly states, captives into slaves, women into subjugated drudges, free peasants into serfs, and the like. No such development lacks excesses, and if kindly rulers did not turn into brutal despots, it would have been miraculous. That we can sit in judgment on these societies, their states, and their oppressive methods is evidence that progress has occurred and, equally importantly, that our circumstances differ profoundly from theirs. Where famine was once a normal feature of life, we today are shocked when no effort is made to feed the starving. But we are shocked only because we have already developed the means to produce a sufficiency, disallowing indifference to scarcity. In short, the circumstances have changed profoundly, however unjust the distribution of the means of life may continue to be. Indeed, that we can even say the distribution is unjust is a verdict that only a society able to eliminate material scarcity—and create, potentially, a postscarcity society—can make.

Thus, our expansive visions of freedom, today, have their preconditions: minimally, technological advancement. Only generations that have not experienced the Great Depression can ignore the preconditional bases for our more generous ideologies. The classical Left, particularly thinkers such as Marx, gave us much systematic thinking on history and contemporary social affairs. But will we elect to follow a truly libertarian use of the resources at our command and create a society that is democratic, communistic, and communalistic, based on popular assemblies, confederations, and sweeping civil liberties? Or will we follow a course that is increasingly statist, centralized, and authoritarian? Here, another "history" or dialectic comes into play—the great traditions of freedom that were elaborated over time by unknown revolutionaries and by libertarian thinkers such as Bakunin, Kropotkin, and Malatesta. We are thus faced with two legacies that have unfolded in tandem with each other: a material one and an ideological one.

Let us be frank and acknowledge that these legacies are not well known or easily understood. But from them, we can weave an ethical approach to social change that can give our endeavors definition and a possibility of success. For one thing, we can declare that "what should be"—humanity's potentialities for freedom, rationality, and self-consciousness—is to be actualized and guide our social lives. We can affirm "what should be" on the basis of decidedly real material possibilities and realizable ideological ones. Knowledge of "what should be," if reason is to guide our behavior, becomes the force driving us to make social change and to produce a rational society. With our material preconditions in place and with reason to guide us to the actualization of our potentialities, we can begin to formulate the concrete steps that a future Left will be obliged to take to achieve its ends. The material preconditions are demonstrably at hand, and reason, fortified by a knowledge of past endeavors to produce a relatively rational society, provides the means to formulate the measures and the means, step by step, to produce a new Left that is relevant for the foreseeable future.

Far from eschewing reason and theory, a future Left that is meaningful must be solidly grounded in theory if it is to have any power to understand the present in relationship to the past, and the future in relationship to the present. A lack of philosophical equipment to interpret events, past and present, will render its theoretical insights fragmentary and bereft of contextuality and continuity. Nor will it be able to show how specific events relate to a larger whole and link them together in a broad perspective. It was this admirable intention, I should note, that induced Marx to give his ideas a systematic and unified form, not any personal disposition on his part for "totalitarianism." The world in which he lived had to be shown that capital accumulation and the bourgeoisie's unrelenting concentration of industrial resources were not products of greed but vital necessities for enterprises in a sharply competitive economy.

One can project an alternative to the present society only by advancing rational alternatives to the existing order of things— alternatives that are objectively and logically based on humanity's potentialities for freedom and innovation. In this respect, the ability of human beings to project themselves beyond their given circumstances, to re-create their world and their social relations, and to infuse innovation with ethical judgments becomes the basis for actualizing a rational society.

This "what should be," as educed by reason, stands on a higher plane of truthfulness and wholeness than does the existential and pragmatic "what is." Figuratively speaking, the contrast between the "what should be" and the "what is," as elaborated and challenged by mind as well as by experience, lies at the heart of dialectic. Indeed, the "what should be," by sitting in judgment on the validity of the given, joins dialectical development in the biosphere with dialectical development in the social sphere. It provides the basis for determining whether a society is rational and to what degree it has rational content. Absent such a criterion, we have no basis for social ethics apart from the egocentric, adventitious, anarchic, and highly subjective statement "I choose!" A social ethics cannot remain suspended in the air without an objective foundation, a comprehensive evolution from the primitive to the increasingly sophisticated, and a coherent content that supports its development.

Moreover, without an objective potentiality (that is, the implicit reality that lends itself to rational eduction, in contrast to mere daydreaming) that sits in "judgment" of existential reality as distinguished from a rationally conceived reality, we have no way to derive an ethics that goes beyond mere personal taste. What is to guide us in understanding the nature of freedom? Why is freedom superior to mere custom or habit? Why is a free society desirable and an enslaved one not, apart from taste and opinion? No social ethics is even possible, let alone desirable, without a processual conception of behavior, from its primal roots in the realm of potentiality at the inception of a human evolution, through that evolution itself, to the level of the rational and discursive. Without criteria supplied by the dialectically derived "ought," the foundations for a revolutionary movement dissolve into an anarchic vacuum of personal choice, the muddled notion that "what is good for me constitutes the good and the true—and that is that!"

As much as we are obliged to deal with the "what is"—with the existential facts of life, including capitalism—it is the dialectically derived "true," as Hegel might put it, that must always remain our guide, precisely because it defines a rational society. Abandon the rational and we are reduced to the level of mere animality from which the course of history and the great struggles of humanity for emancipation have tended to free us. It is to break faith with History, conceived as a rational development toward freedom and innovation, and to diminish the defining standards of our humanity. If we often seem adrift, it is not for lack of a compass and a map by which to guide ourselves toward the actualization of our uniquely human and social potentialities.

This leads us to another premise for acquiring social truth: the importance of dialectical thinking as our compass. This logic constitutes both the method and the substance of an eductive process of reasoning and unfolding. Eduction is the procedure that immanently elicits the implicit traits that lend themselves to rational actualization, namely, freedom and innovation. A deep ecologist once challenged me by asking why freedom should be more desirable than unfreedom. I reply that freedom, as it develops objectively through various phases of the ascent of life, from mere choice as a form of self-maintenance to the re-creation of the environment by intellection and innovation, can make for a world that is more habitable, humane, and creative than anything achieved by the interplay of natural forces. Indeed, to rephrase a famous axiom of Hegel's, a point can be reached in a free society where what is not free is not real (or actual).

Indeed, a task of dialectical thinking is to separate the rational from the arbitrary, external, and adventitious in which it unfolds, an endeavor that demands considerable intellectual courage as well as insight. Thus, the conquests of Alexander the Great dovetail with the rational movement of History, insofar as Alexander unified a decomposing world made up of rotting city-states and parasitic monarchies and transmitted Hellenic thought to it. But the explosion of Mongol horsemen from the steppes of central Asia contributed no more to the rational course of events than did, say, a decline in rainfall over North Africa that turned a vast forested area into a grim, formidable desert. Moreover, to speak of a Mongol invasion as evidence of a "potentiality for evil" is to divest the rich philosophical term *potentiality* of its creative content. Much better to use here the ideologically neutral term *capacity*, which can be applied anywhere for any phenomenon—and to no intelligible purpose whatever.

Remote as it may seem to some, dialectical thinking is, in my view, indispensable for creating the map and formulating the agenda for a new Left. The actualization of humanity's potentiality for a rational society—the "what should be" achieved by human development—occurs in the fully democratic municipality, the municipality based on a face-to-face democratic assembly composed of free citizens, for whom the word politics means direct popular control over the community's public affairs by means of democratic institutions. Such a system of control should occur within the framework of a duly constituted system of laws, rationally derived by discourse, experience, historical knowledge, and judgment. The free municipality, in effect, is not only a sphere for deploying political tactics but a product of reason. Here, means and ends are in perfect congruence, without the troubling "transitions" that once gave us a "dictatorship of the proletariat" that soon turned into a dictatorship of the party.

Furthermore, the libertarian municipality, like any social artifact, is constituted. It is to be consciously created by the exercise of reason, not by arbitrary "choices" that lack objective ethical criteria and therefore may easily yield oppressive institutions and chaotic communities. The municipality's constitution and laws should define the duties as well as the rights of the citizen, that is, they should explicitly clarify the realm of necessity as well as the realm of freedom. The life of the municipality is determined by laws, not arbitrarily "by men." Law, as such, is not necessarily oppressive: indeed, for thousands of years the oppressed demanded laws, as *nomos*, to prevent arbitrary rule and the "tyranny of structurelessness." In the free municipality, law must always be rationally, discursively, and openly derived and subject to careful consideration. At the same time, we must continually be aware of regulations and definitions that have harnessed humanity to their oppressors.

As Rousseau saw, the municipality is not merely an agglomeration of buildings but of free citizens. Combined with reason, order can yield coherent institutions. Lacking order and reason, we are left with a system of arbitrary rule, with controls that are not accountable or answerable to the people—in short, with tyranny. What constitutes a state is not the existence of institutions but rather the existence of professional institutions, set apart from the people, that are designed to dominate them for the express purpose of securing their oppression in one form or another.

A revolutionary politics does not challenge the existence of institutions as such but rather assesses whether a given institution is emancipatory and rational or oppressive and irrational. The growing proclivity in oppositional movements to transgress institutions and laws merely because they exist is in fact reactionary and, in any case, serves to divert public attention away from the need to create or transform institutions into democratic, popular, and rational entities. A "politics" of disorder or "creative chaos," or a naïve practice of "taking over the streets" (usually little more than a street festival), regresses participants to the behavior of a juvenile herd; by replacing the rational with the "primal" or "playful," it abandons the Enlightenment's commitment to the civilized, the cultivated, and the knowledgeable. Joyful as revolutions may sometimes also be, they are primarily earnestly serious and even bloody; and if they are not systematic and astutely led, they will invariably end in counterrevolution and terror. The Communards of 1871 may have been deliriously drunk when they "stormed the heavens" (as Marx put it), but when they sobered up, they found that the walls surrounding Paris had been breached by the counterrevolutionary Versaillais. After a week of fighting, their resistance collapsed, and the Versaillais shot them arbitrarily and in batches by the thousands. A politics that lacks sufficient seriousness in its core behavior may make for wonderful Anarchy but is disastrous revolutionism.

What specific political conclusions do these observations yield? What political agenda do they support?

First, the "what should be" should preside over every tenet of a future political agenda and movement. As important as a politics of protest may be, it is no substitute for a politics of social innovation. Today, Marxists and anarchists alike tend to behave defensively, merely reacting to the existing social order and to the problems it creates. Capitalism thus orchestrates the behavior of its intuitive opponents. Moreover, it has learned to mute opposition by shrewdly making partial concessions to protesters.

The municipality, as we have seen, is the authentic terrain for the actualization of humanity's social potentialities to be free and innovative. Still, left to itself, even the most emancipated municipality may become parochial, insular, and narrow. Confederalism remains at once the operational means of rounding out deficits that any municipality is likely to face when it introduces a libertarian communist economy. Few, if any, municipalities are capable of meeting their needs on their own. An attempt to achieve economic autarchy—and the concomitant cultural parochialism that it so often yields in less economically developed societies—would be socially undesirable. Nor does the mere exchange of surplus products remove the commodity relationship; the sharing of goods according to a truly libertarian view is far different from an exchange of goods, which closely resembles market exchanges. By what standard would the "value" of surplus commodities be determined—by their congealed labor? The incipient bases for a capitalist economy remained unrecognized, even in anarchist Catalonia, among those who boasted of their communist convictions.

Still another distinction that must be drawn is that between policymaking decisions and strictly administrative ones. Just as the problems of distribution must not be permitted to drag a community into capitalist mores and market practices, administrators must not be allowed to make policy decisions, which properly belong to popular assemblies. Such practices must be made, quite simply, illegal, that is, the community must establish regulations, with punitive features, forbidding committees and agencies to exercise rights that properly belong to the assembled community. As insensitive as such measures may seem to delicate libertarian sensibilities, they are justified by a history in which hard-won rights were slowly eroded by elites who sought privileges for themselves at the expense of the many. Postscarcity in the availability of the means of life may serve to render any pursuit of economic privilege a laughable anachronism. But, as hierarchical society has shown, something more than economic privileges, such as the enhancement of status and power, may be involved.

Human beings actualize their potentialities in free municipalities that are rationally and discursively constituted and institutionalized in free popular assemblies. Whatever politics abets this development is historically progressive; any self-professed politics that diminishes this development is reactionary and reinforces the existing social order. Mere expressions of formless "community" that devolve into "street festivals," particularly when they become substitutes for a libertarian municipalist politics (or, more disturbingly, a distortion of them), feed the overall juvenilization that capitalism promotes through its impetus to dumb down society on a massive scale.

During the interwar years, when proactive forces for revolutionary change seemed to threaten the very existence of the social order, the classical Left was focused on a distinct set of issues: the need for a planned economy, the problems of a chronic economic crisis, the imminence of a worldwide war, the advance of fascism, and the challenging examples provided by the Russian Revolution. Today, contemporary leftists are more focused on major ecological dislocations, corporate gigantism, the influence of technology on daily life, and the impact of the mass media. The classical Left looked at deep-seated crises and the feasibility of revolutionary approaches to create social change; the contemporary Left is more attentive to a different set of abuses.

The capitalism under which we live today is far removed from the capitalism that Marx knew and that revolutionaries of all kinds tried to overthrow in the first half of the twentieth century. It has, indeed, developed in great part along the lines Marx suggested in his closing chapters of the first volume of *Capital*: as an economy whose very law of life is accumulation, concentration, and expansion. When it can no longer develop along these lines, it will cease to be capitalism. This follows from the very logic of commodity exchange, with its expression in competition and technological innovation.

Marxist productivism and anarchist individualism have both led to blind alleys, albeit widely divergent ones. Where Marxism tends to overorganize people into parties, unions, and proletarian "armies" guided by elitist leaders, anarchism eschews organization and leaders as "vanguards" and celebrates revolutionism as an instinctive impulse unguided by reason or theory. Where Marxism celebrates technological advances, without placing them in a rational, ethical, and ecological context, anarchism deprecates sophisticated technics as the demonic parent of the "technocratic man," who is lured to perdition by reason and civilization. Technophilia has been pitted against technophobia; analytical reason against raw instinct; and a synthetic civilization against a presumably primeval nature.

The future of the Left, in the last analysis, depends upon its ability to accept what is valid in both Marxism and anarchism for the present time and for the future that is coming into view. In an era of permanent technological revolution, the validity of a theory and a movement will depend profoundly on how clearly it can see what lies just ahead. Radically new technologies, still difficult to imagine, will undoubtedly be introduced that will have a transformative effect upon the entire world. New power alignments may arise that produce a degree of social disequilibrium that has not been seen for decades, accompanied by new weapons of unspeakable homicidal and ecocidal effects, and a continuing ecological crisis.

But no greater damage could afflict human consciousness than the loss of the Enlightenment program: the advance of reason, knowledge, science, ethics, and even technics, which must be modulated to find a progressive place in a free and humane society. Without the attainments of the Enlightenment, no libertarian revolutionary consciousness is possible. In assessing the revolutionary tradition, a reasoned Left has to shake off dead traditions that, as Marx warned, weigh on the heads of the living, and commit itself to create a rational society and a rounded civilization.

December 2002

Acknowledgements

Some of these essays appeared previously in other venues and we would like to acknowledge them as follows: The essay "The Ecological Crisis and the Need to Remake Society" was originally written for a Greek audience in 1992 and later published in English under the title "The Ecological Crisis, Socialism, and the Need to Remake Society" in the journal *Society and Nature* vol. 2, no. 3, 1994. "A Politics for the Twenty-First Century" was originally a video-transmitted speech presented to the First International Conference on Libertarian Municipalism, Lisbon, 1998. "The Meaning of Confederalism" was originally published in *From Urbanization to Cities*, London: Cassell, 1995. "Libertarian Municipalism: A Politics of Direct Democracy" was originally titled "Libertarian Municipalism: An Overview" and appeared in Green Perspectives, no. 24, 1991. "Cities: The Unfolding of Reason in History" was excerpted from the article, "Comments on the International Social Ecology Network Gathering and the 'Deep Social Ecology' of John Clark" published in *Democracy and Nature*, vol. 3, no. 3, 1997. "Nationalism and the 'National Question'" was originally published in *Society and Nature* vol. 2, no. 2, 1994. "Anarchism and Power in the Spanish Revolution" appeared in *Communalism*, no. 2, 2002.

We gratefully acknowledge Audrea Lim, Jacob Stevens, Mark

Martin, and the entire team at Verso for their tireless efforts in disseminating radical thought. We want to also acknowledge the longstanding dedication to these ideas by everyone at the Institute for Social Ecology. Finally, Jim Schumacher has supported Murray Bookchin and his work in ways that go far beyond the love and loyalty of a typical son-in-law; his commitment to Murray's vision and legacy were invaluable in the realization of this volume.

Further Reading

BOOKS BY MURRAY BOOKCHIN

Post-Scarcity Anarchism. Berkeley: Ramparts Press, 1971; and Oakland: AK Press, 2004.

The Limits of the City. New York: Harper and Row, 1974.

The Spanish Anarchists: The Heroic Years 1868-1936. New York: Free Life Editions, 1977; and San Fransisco: AK Press, 2001.

Toward an Ecological Society. Montreal: Black Rose Books, 1980.

The Ecology of Freedom. Palo Alto: Cheshire Books, 1982; and San Francisco: AK Press, 2001.

The Modern Crisis. Philadelphia: New Society Publishers, 1986; Montreal: Black Rose Books, 1987.

The Rise of Urbanization and the Decline of Citizenship. San Francisco: Sierra Club Books, 1987. Revised edition as *From Urbanization to Cities: Towards a New Politics of Citizenship*. London: Cassell, 1995.

Remaking Society: Paths to a Green Future. Boston: South End Press, 1990.

The Philosophy of Social Ecology: Essays on Dialectical Naturalism. Montreal: Black Rose Books, 1990.

Defending the Earth: A Dialogue Between Murray Bookchin and Dave

Foreman, coauthored with Dave Foreman. Boston: South End Press, 1991.

Which Way for the Ecology Movement? San Francisco: AK Press, 1994.

To Remember Spain: The Anarchist and Syndicalist Revolution of 1936. San Francisco: AK Press, 1994.

Re-Enchanting Humanity: A Defense of the Human Spirit Against Anti-Humanism, Misanthropy, Mysticism, and Primitivism. New York: Cassell, 1995.

Social Anarchism or Lifestyle Anarchism: An Unbridgeable Chasm. San Francisco: AK Press, 1995.

The Third Revolution: Popular Movements in the Revolutionary Era. New York: Cassell, Vol. 1, 1996; Vol. 2, 1998. London: Continuum, Vol. 3, 2004; Vol. 4, 2005.

Anarchism, Marxism and the Future of the Left. San Francisco: AK Press, 1999.

Social Ecology and Communalism. Oakland: AK Press, 2007.

The Politics of Cosmology. Forthcoming.

The Murray Bookchin Reader. Forthcoming.

Herber, Lewis (pseudonym), *Our Synthetic Environment.* New York: Alfred A. Knopf, 1962.

Herber, Lewis (pseudonym), *Crisis in Our Cities.* Englewood Cliffs, NJ: Prentice Hall, 1965.

BOOKS ABOUT MURRAY BOOKCHIN

White, Damian, *Bookchin: A Critical Appraisal.* London: Pluto Press, 2008.

Price, Andy, *Recovering Bookchin: Social Ecology and the Crises of Our Time.* Porsgrunn, Norway: New Compass Press, 2012.

Printed in the United States
by Baker & Taylor Publisher Services